Prisoners of Our Thoughts

Prisoners of Our Thoughts

**Viktor Frankl's
Principles at Work**

Alex Pattakos

BERRETT-KOEHLER PUBLISHERS, INC.
San Francisco

Berrett-Koehler Publishers, Inc.
235 Montgomery Street, Suite 650
San Francisco, CA 94104-2916
Tel: (415) 288-0260   Fax: (415) 362-2512   www.bkconnection.com

Ordering Information

Quantity sales. Special discounts are available on quantity purchases by corporations, associations, and others. For details, contact the "Special Sales Department" at the Berrett-Koehler address above.

Individual sales. Berrett-Koehler publications are available through most bookstores. They can also be ordered direct from Berrett-Koehler: Tel: (800) 929-2929;
Fax: (802) 864-7626; www.bkconnection.com

Orders for college textbook/course adoption use. Please contact
Berrett-Koehler: Tel: (800) 929-2929; Fax: (802) 864-7626.

Orders by U.S. trade bookstores and wholesalers. Please contact
Publishers Group West, 1700 Fourth Street, Berkeley, CA 94710.
Tel: (510) 528-1444; Fax (510) 528-3444.

Berrett-Koehler and the BK logo are registered trademarks of Berrett-Koehler Publishers, Inc.

Printed in the United States of America

Berrett-Koehler books are printed on long-lasting acid-free paper. When it is available, we choose paper that has been manufactured by environmentally responsible processes. These may include using trees grown in sustainable forests, incorporating recycled paper, minimizing chlorine in bleaching, or recycling the energy produced at the paper mill.

Library of Congress Cataloging-in-Publication Data
Pattakos, Alex
  Prisoners of our thoughts : Viktor Frankl's principles at work / Alex Pattakos.
    p. cm.
  Includes bibliographical references and index.
  ISBN-10: 1-57675-288-7; ISBN-13: 978-1-57675-288-3
      1. Frankl, Viktor Emil.   2. Conduct of life.   3. Logotherapy.   4. Psychotherapy.
I. Title.
RC440.5.P38 2004
616.89'14—dc22   2004047714

FIRST EDITION
09 08 07   10 9 8 7 6 5

Text design by Detta Penna

Contents

Why do some people seem to have an easier time dealing with complex and challenging situations than others? Why do some people seem more capable of dealing with change than others?

Applying the therapeutic system of world-renowned psychiatrist and philosopher, Viktor E. Frankl, to work and the workplace, learn how to bring personal meaning and fulfillment to your work and everyday life and achieve your highest potential!

Core Principles

1 *Exercise the freedom to choose your attitude*—in all situations, no matter how desperate they may appear or actually be, you always have the ultimate freedom to choose your attitude.

2 *Realize your will to meaning*—commit authentically to meaningful values and goals that only you can actualize and fulfill.

3 *Detect the meaning of life's moments*—only you can answer for your own life by detecting the meaning at any given moment and assuming responsibility for weaving your unique tapestry of existence.

4 *Don't work against yourself*—avoid becoming so obsessed with or fixated on an intent or outcome that you actually work against the desired result.

5 *Look at yourself from a distance*—only human beings possess the capacity to look at themselves out of some perspective or distance, including the uniquely human trait known as your "sense of humor."

6 *Shift your focus of attention*—deflect your attention from the problem situation to something else and build your coping mechanisms for dealing with stress and change.

7 *Extend beyond yourself*—manifest the human spirit at work by relating and being directed to something more than yourself.

Foreword

Stephen R. Covey

Shortly before Viktor Frankl's passing in September 1997, I had heard of his declining health, illness, and hospitalization. I was very anxious to talk with him so that I could express my profound gratitude for his life's work—for his impact on millions of people, including my own life and life's work. I understood that he had lost his sight and that his wife was reading to him several hours each day in the hospital. I will never forget the feeling of hearing his voice and visiting with him. He was so kind and gracious as he listened to my expressions of appreciation, esteem, and love. I felt as if I were speaking to a great and noble spirit. After patiently listening, he said, "Stephen, you talk to me as if I am ready to check out. I still have two important projects I need to complete." How true to form! How true to character! How true to the principles of Logotherapy!

Frankl's desire and determination to continue to contribute reminded me of his collaborative work with Dr. Hans Selye of Montreal, Canada—famous for his research and writings on stress. Selye taught that it is only when we have meaningful work and projects that our immune system is strengthened and the degenerative aging forces are slowed down. He called this kind of stress "eustress" rather than distress, which comes from a life without meaning and integrity. I'm sure these two souls influenced each other, reinforcing both the physical and psychological benefits of Logotherapy, of man's search for meaning.

When Alex Pattakos graciously invited me to write a foreword to *Prisoners of Our Thoughts* and told me that the Frankl family had suggested this to him, I was both honored and excited to participate—particularly since they felt my work with organizations in management and leadership beautifully paralleled Viktor Frankl's "principles at work," the heart of this splendid book. My sense of the significance of this book deepened further when Pattakos wrote me, "A year before he died, I was sitting with Dr. Frankl in his study and he grabbed my arm and said, 'Alex, yours is the book that needs to be written!'"

I will never forget how deeply moved and inspired I was in the sixties when I studied *Man's Search for Meaning* and also *The Doctor and the Soul*. These two books, along with Frankl's other writings and lectures, reaffirmed "my soul's code" regarding our power of choice, our unique endowment of self-awareness, and our essence, our will for meaning. While on a writing sabbatical in Hawaii and in a very reflective state of mind, I was wandering through the stacks of a university library and picked up a book. I read the following three lines, which literally staggered me and again reaffirmed Frankl's essential teachings:

> Between stimulus and response, there is a space.
> In that space lies our freedom and our power to choose our response.
> In our response lies our growth and our happiness.

I did not note the name of the author, so I've never been able to give proper attribution. On a later trip to Hawaii I even went back to find the source and found the library building itself was no longer present.

The space between what happens to us and our response, our freedom to choose that response and the impact it can have upon our lives, beautifully illustrate that we can become a product of our decisions, not our conditions. They illustrate the three values that Frankl continually taught: the creative value; the experiential value; and the attitudinal value. We have the power to choose our response to our circumstances. We have the power to shape our circumstances; indeed, we have the responsibility, and if we ignore this space, this freedom, this responsibility, the essence of our life and our legacy could be frustrated.

One time I was leaving a military base where I had been teaching principle-centered leadership over a period of time. As I was saying goodbye to the commander of that base, a colonel, I asked him, "Why would you undertake such a significant change effort to bring principle-centered living and leadership to your command when you know full well you will be swimming upstream against powerful cultural forces? You are in your thirtieth year and you are retiring at the end of this year. You have had a successful military career and you could simply maintain the successful pattern you've had and go into your retirement with all of the honors and the plaudits that come with your dedicated years of service." His answer was unforgettable. It seared itself into my soul. He said, "Recently, my father passed away. Knowing that he was dying, he called my mother and myself to his bedside. He motioned to me to come close to him so that he could whisper something in my ear. My mother stood by, watching in tears. My father said, 'Son, promise me you won't do life like I did. Son, I didn't do right by you or by your mother, and I never really made a difference. Son, promise me you won't do life like I did.'"

This military commander said, "Stephen, that is why I am undertaking this change effort. That is why I want to bring our whole command to an entirely new level of performance and contribution. I want to make a difference, and for the first time I sincerely hope that my successors do better than I have. Up to this point, I had hoped that I would be the high-water mark, but no longer. I want to get these principles so institutionalized and so built into our culture that they will be sustainable and go on and on. I know it will be a struggle. I may even ask for an extension so that I can continue to see this work through, but I want to honor the greatest legacy that my father ever gave me, and that is the desire to make a difference."

From this commander we learn that courage is not the absence of fear but the awareness there is something more important. We spend at least a third of our life either preparing for work or doing work, usually inside organizations. Even our retirement should be filled with meaningful projects, inside organizations or families or societies. Work and love essentially comprise the essence of mortality.

The great humanistic psychologist, Abraham Maslow, came to similar thoughts near the end of his life, which essentially affirmed Frankl's "will to meaning" theme. He felt that his own need hierarchy theory was too needs determined and that self-actualization was not the highest need. In the end, he concluded that self-transcendence was the human soul's highest need, which reflected more the spirit of Frankl. Maslow's wife, Bertha, and his research associate put together his final thinking along these lines in the book, *The Farther Reaches of Human Nature*.

My own work with organizations and with people in the world of work focuses a great deal on developing personal and organizational mission statements. I have found that when you get enough people interacting freely and synergistically, and when these people are informed about the realities of their industry or profession and their own culture, they begin to tap into a kind of collective conscience and awareness of the need to add value, to really leave a legacy, and they set up value guidelines to fulfill that legacy. Ends and means are inseparable; in fact, the ends pre-exist in the means. No worthy end can ever really be accomplished with unworthy means.

I have found in my teaching that the single most exhilarating, thrilling, and motivating idea that people have ever really seriously contemplated is the idea of the power of choice—the idea that the best way to predict their future is to create it. It is basically the idea of personal freedom, of learning to ask Viktor Frankl's question: What is life asking of me? What is this situation asking of me? It's more freedom *to* rather than freedom *from*. It's definitely an inside-out rather than an outside-in approach.

I have found that when people get caught up in this awareness, this kind of mindfulness, and if they genuinely ask such questions and consult their conscience, almost always the purposes and values they come up with are transcendent—that is, they deal with meaning that is larger than their own life, one that truly adds value and contributes to other people's lives—the kinds of things that Viktor Frankl did in the death camps of Nazi Germany. They break cycles; they establish new cycles, new positive energies. They become what I like to call "transition figures"—people who break with past cultural mindless patterns of behavior and attitude.

The range of what we see and do
Is limited by what we fail to notice.
And because we fail to notice
That we fail to notice,
There is little we can do
To change
Until we notice
How failing to notice
Shapes our thoughts and deeds.
　　　—R.D. Laing

With this kind of thinking and with the seven magnificent principles Dr. Pattakos describes in this important book, a kind of primary greatness is developed where character and contribution, conscience and love, choice and meaning, all have their play and synergy with each other. This is contrasted with secondary greatness, described in the last chapter of this book—being those who are successful in society's eyes but personally unfulfilled.

Finally, let me suggest two ideas on how to get the very most from this book. First, share or teach the core principles, one by one, to those you live with and work around who might be interested. Second, live them. To learn something but not to do is really not to learn. To know something but not to do is really not to know. Otherwise, if we just intellectualize these core principles and verbalize them, but do not share and practice them, we would be like a person who is blind from birth explaining to another what it means to see, based on an academic study of light, its properties, the eye and its anatomy. As you read this book, I challenge you to experience the freedom to choose your own attitude, to exercise your will to meaning, to detect the meaning of life's moments, to not work against yourself, to look at yourself from a distance, and to shift your focus of attention and extend beyond yourself. I suggest you consider learning this material sequentially, just by reading the principle, teaching it and applying it, then reading the next one, and so forth. You may want to simply read the entire book all at once to give yourself the overview, and then go back and learn them sequentially through your own experiencing. You will become a change catalyst. You will become a transition figure. You will stop bad cycles and start good ones. Life will take on a meaning as you've never known it before. I know this is so from my own experiences and from working with countless organizations and individuals in the world of work.

As my grandfather taught me, and as Viktor Frankl taught me, life is a mission, not a career.

This book is dedicated to
Viktor E. Frankl, MD, PhD (1905–1997),
whose life and legacy will forever bring light to darkness,
and
to my partner in the search for meaning,
Elaine, whose love and support will forever
bring warmth to the meaning of life.

Preface

Have you ever worked in a job that you really didn't like? Or even if you were satisfied with your job—say, because it paid well or seemed secure—you still didn't feel fulfilled by the work that you were doing? More broadly, have you ever wondered if there was more to "life" than what you were experiencing? Have you ever felt like "bad" things just happened to you, challenging situations that were out of your control? If you answered yes to any of these questions, or even asked yourself such questions before now, you should know that you are not alone. Not at all. And, importantly, you should know that, because we're all human, it is totally natural to ask ourselves such fundamental questions about the way we work and live.

This book deals with the human quest for meaning and, therefore, was written with you in mind. It is grounded firmly in the philosophy and approach of the world-renowned psychiatrist, Viktor Frankl, author of the classic bestseller, *Man's Search for Meaning* (named one of the ten most influential books in America by the Library of Congress). Frankl, a survivor of the Nazi concentration camps during World War II, is the founder of Logotherapy, a meaning-centered and humanistic approach to psychotherapy. His ideas and experiences related to the search for meaning have significantly influenced people around the world. In this book, you will find a conceptual foundation, as well as practical guidance, for examining your own questions about meaning in your work and everyday life.

The goal of this book, moreover, is to bring meaning to work—that is, to do for the domain of work what Frankl, as a psychiatrist, was able to do for psychotherapy. Because I am defining the notion of "work" very broadly, the message in this book applies to a very broad audience as well. In fact, it applies to volunteers as well as to paid workers; to people working in all sectors and industries; to retirees; to individuals beginning a job search or career; and to those in "transition." And, because this book demonstrates how Frankl's principles actually *work* in a generic context, its message can be applied to everyday living too. In this regard, besides introducing you to Frankl's core ideas about life, the book is filled with examples, stories, exercises, and practical tools that can help guide you on your path to finding meaning at work *and* in your personal life.

It was in a meeting with Frankl at his home in Vienna, Austria, in August 1996, when I first proposed the idea of writing a book that would apply his core principles and approach explicitly to work and the workplace, to the world of business. Frankl was more than encouraging when, in his typically direct and passionate style, he leaned across his desk, grabbed my arm, and said: "Alex, yours is the book that *needs* to be written!" As you can imagine, I felt that Frankl's words had been branded into the core of my being, and I was determined, from that moment forward, to make this book idea a reality. And so it is.

My fascination with Frankl and his work, like so many

The author with Dr. Frankl in his study, Vienna, Austria, August 1996

other people's, is long-standing. Yes, I feel blessed that I was given the opportunity to meet with him in person and seek his counsel. This said, Frankl's influence on my work and personal life go back almost forty years. I have spent many of these years studying his groundbreaking work in existential analysis, Logotherapy, and the search for meaning, and have applied his principles in many different work environments and situations. As a mental health professional, my reliance on the power of Frankl's ideas has evolved and expanded over time. In this regard, I have employed (and tested) various elements of his philosophy and approach within a wide variety of organizational settings, as well as having worked closely with many individuals in the throes of an existential dilemma either at work or in their personal lives. During this time, of course, I also reflected seriously on my own life journey and found myself, on numerous occasions, relying on and benefiting from Frankl's wisdom. You'll find some of my own meaning-focused challenges and opportunities described in this book.

It is important to underscore that Viktor Frankl, throughout his life, "practiced what he preached." This, I must say from personal experience, is not always easy to do.

There is a saying in the academic world suggesting that we teach in order to learn, that is, we don't know what we don't know until we try to teach it. The same thing can be said about writing a book. In many respects, *writing* a book is the easy part. The really hard part, I must confess, comes when we try to *do* what we write about. Frankl was able to do both; he lived and worked with meaning all of his life. I can only try to follow his lead and hope that, by writing "the book that *needs* to be written," I have also learned how to live and work with meaning.

I also must say that the same thing applies to you. After you read this book, I challenge you *not* to put it out of sight, out of mind. No, please don't do that, because I've distilled some core principles from Frankl's voluminous body of work that deserve more of your attention than a simple read-through will provide. After reading this book, I would like you to "live" it by practicing the exercises, reviewing the concepts and cases (as many times as might be necessary for you), and adopting the core principles in your daily work and life. Only in this way will this book be more than another book in your library. Only in this way will this book help you find true meaning in your work and life. And only in this way will the message that Frankl branded in my soul,— "Alex, yours is the book that *needs* to be written!"—have the kind of meaning that he intended.

Alex Pattakos
Santa Fe, New Mexico USA
August 2004

Acknowledgements

If ever a book was more a process than a product, then this must be it. And throughout the process many people contributed, in many meaningful ways, to bringing the final product into being. So many, in fact, that I cannot begin to name them all. Yet, some people were especially important in this project—coming to my aid at critical moments in the process—and therefore I would like for them to know how thankful I am for their involvement.

Elaine, my wife and business partner, who stood by me through thick and thin, and who helped to keep the flame burning so that this book would get to see the light of day. No words could thank you enough; thanks for being you and for the many, many ways that you contributed to this book.

The Frankl family, who believed in and supported this book project from the beginning. I am forever grateful.

Steve Piersanti, publisher, and Jeevan Sivasubramani-am, managing editor, Berrett-Koehler Publishers, for not giving up on me or this book over so many years, and for ensuring that it was the best product possible.

The entire team at Berrett-Koehler Publishers for believing that the search for meaning at work is more than a book.

All my fellow Berrett-Koehler authors, who share a common outlook on "creating a world that works for all"; individually and collectively, thanks for making a difference.

Janet Thomas, who worked hard to turn my ideas into prose and who contributed a writing perspective and expertise that will never be forgotten.

The various reviewers of my manuscript, at different stages, who not only helped to improve the final product but also taught me a lot about myself in the process.

Patti Havenga-Coetzer, friend and colleague, who always keeps Viktor Frankl's spirit alive and well in her heart.

Jeffrey Zeig, for helping to ensure that Viktor Frankl's legacy lives forever.

My clients and students over the years, who helped me, by sharing their thoughts and experiences, to express and practice the ideas that are now in this book.

Finally, I want to thank all my other friends, colleagues, and extended family for their encouragement of my work, even if they didn't quite understand what I was doing when I told them that I was on a "search for meaning."

Life Doesn't Just Happen to Us

Ultimately, man should not ask what the meaning of his life is, but rather must recognize that it is he who is asked. In a word, each man is questioned by life; and he can only answer to life by answering for his own life; to life he can only respond by being responsible. [1]

Every day, Vita delivers my mail—cheerfully. It's her trademark attitude. One day, in lousy weather, I heard her whistling as she went about doing her deliveries. Instinctively I shouted out to her, "Thank you for doing such a great job." She stopped dead in her tracks with surprise. "Thank *you*," she said. "Wow, I'm not accustomed to hearing such words. I really appreciate it."

I wanted to know more. "How do you stay so positive and upbeat about delivering mail every day?" I asked her.

"I don't just deliver mail," she said. "I see myself helping to connect people to other people. I help build the community. Besides, people depend on me and I don't want to let them down." Her response was enthusiastic and proud.

Vita's attitude about her work reflected the words inscribed on the General Post Office building in New York

City: *Neither snow nor rain nor gloom of night stays these couriers from the swift completion of their appointed rounds.* It was the Greek historian Herodotus who wrote these words in the fifth century B.C. The ancient delivery of messages from one person to another is at the very heart of our Information Age; yet these days, it's the phrase "going postal" that we're more likely to recognize.

Fair or unfair, "going postal" has become the symbol of all the negativity a job has to offer: boredom, repetitiveness, exposure to the elements, dangerous dogs, irritated customers, and a kind of automated behavior that ultimately inspires an explosion of pent-up rage—a killing spree, retaliation against all the suffered injustice of the job.

> *What threatens contemporary man is the alleged meaninglessness of his life, or, as I call it, the existential vacuum within him. And when does this vacuum open up, when does this so often latent vacuum become manifest? In the state of boredom.* [2]

No matter what our opinions might be about the stature of any career or profession, it is the person doing the job that gives the job meaning. Vita is proof that those ancient words of Herodotus are alive and well in the twenty-first century.

But Vita's attitude goes beyond the "swift completion of her appointed rounds" (to paraphrase Herodotus). She experiences her work as serving a higher purpose. Her attitude about her job, and its "drudgery," goes far beyond an exercise in positive thinking. Vita sees her mail delivery responsibility as a personal, life-saving mission, one that could be fulfilled by her, and only by her. She knows she is depended on, perhaps even by people who feel disdain for her work, and it means something. She brings meaning to her job, and in turn, it becomes meaningful.

I am convinced that, in the final analysis, there is no situation which does not contain the seed of meaning.[3]

Why is it that some people, like Vita my mail carrier, experience their work—even mundane work—with passion and commitment? Why do some people have an easier time dealing with complex and challenging situations at work and in life? Why do some people deal more easily with change? Why do some people find meaning and fulfillment in their work and everyday life, while others do not? There are no simple answers to these complex questions; but there are meaningful answers. That is the goal of this book: to illuminate the search for meaning, as a path to meaning, whether in our work or in our everyday lives.

What This Book Is About

We are, by nature, creatures of habit. Searching for a life that is both predictable and within our "comfort zone," we rely on routine and, for the most part, learned thinking patterns. In effect, we create pathways in our minds in much the same way that a path is beaten through a grass field from repeated use. And because these patterns are automatic, we may believe these habitual ways of thinking and behaving to be "beyond our control." Life, it seems, just happens to us. Not only do we rationalize our responses to life but we also fall prey to forces that work to limit our potential as human beings. By viewing ourselves as relatively powerless and driven by our instincts, the possibility that we create, or at least *co-create*, our own reality becomes difficult to grasp. Instead, we lock ourselves inside our own mental prisons. We lose sight of our own natural potential, as well as that of others.

> Each of us has his own inner concentration camp . . . we must deal with, with forgiveness and patience—as full human beings; as we are and what we will become.[4]

The ways in which we hold ourselves "prisoners of our thoughts" are well documented in the work of many who explore the landscape of our psycho-spiritual lives. Physician Deepak Chopra, in the audiotape of his book *Unconditional Life*, says "We erect and build a prison, and the tragedy is that we cannot even see the walls of this prison."[5]

It is through our own search for meaning that we are able to reshape our patterns of thinking, "unfreeze" ourselves from our limited perspective, find the key, and unlock the door of our metaphorical prison cell.

Viktor Frankl, a psychiatrist who suffered through imprisonment in Nazi concentration camps during World War II, found meaning because of, and in spite of, the suffering all around him. His life's work resulted in the therapeutic approach called *Logotherapy*, which paved the way for us to know meaning as a foundation of our existence. Frankl is quick to say, however, that such traumatic suffering is *not* a prerequisite for finding meaning in our lives. He means that even if and when we do suffer, no matter what the severity, we have the ability to find meaning in the situation. Choosing to do so is the path to a meaningful life. And a meaningful life includes meaningful work.

This book explores seven Core Principles that I have

derived from Frankl's work: (1) we are free to choose our attitude toward everything that happens to us; (2) we can realize our will to meaning by making a conscious commitment to meaningful values and goals; (3) we can find meaning in all of life's moments; (4) we can learn to see how we work against ourselves; (5) we can look at ourselves from a distance and gain insight and perspective as well as laugh at ourselves; (6) we can shift our focus of attention when coping with difficult situations; and (7) we can reach out beyond ourselves and make a difference in the world. These seven principles, which I believe form the foundation of Frankl's work, are available to us anytime, all the time. They lead us to meaning, to freedom, and to deep connection to our own lives as well as to the lives of others in our local and global communities.

Viewing life as inherently meaningful and literally unlimited in potential requires a shift in consciousness. It also requires responsible action on our part for, as Frankl points out, the potential for meaning that exists in each moment of life can only be searched for and detected by each of us individually. This responsibility, he says, is "to be actualized by each of us at any time, even in the most miserable situations and literally up to the last breath of ourselves."[6]

Frankl walked this path completely. By living a life with meaning right up to his last breath, he showed us how his philosophy and therapeutic approach were grounded in practice. His personal experiences throughout his long life, both as a survivor of the Nazi death camps and as a revered and respected thought leader, serve to illuminate the unlimited potential of a human being. His life gives us rich and ample evidence that the keys to freedom from life's "prison cells"—real and imagined—are within, and within reach.

Whether we choose this path of liberation, however, is a decision that only we as individuals can make and for which only we can be held responsible. When we search out and discover the authentic meaning of our existence and our experiences, we discover that life doesn't happen *to* us. *We* happen to life; and *we* make it meaningful.

Humanizing Work

The transformation of work in the twenty-first century is, in many respects, a *call for humanity*—a new consciousness that suggests more than simply trying to strike a balance between our work and our personal life. It is a call to honor our own individuality and fully engage our human spirit at work— wherever that may be. While this idea of empowering workers in body, mind, and spirit is not new, actually putting it to work *is* new. In some ways, our technological advances have redesigned work to better accommodate *human* factors. What we need now is a way to elevate the *human spirit* at work.

The goal of this book is to bring meaning to work and, quite frankly, to do for the phenomenon of work what Frankl as a psychiatrist was able to do for psychotherapy. His unique approach is internationally recognized as a system of humanistic psychotherapy and Frankl himself has been referred to by some as the founder of humanistic medicine and psychiatry. Logotherapy, in short, seeks *to make us aware of our freedom of response to all aspects of our destiny.* This humanistic view of psychotherapy helps clients to find concrete meaning in their lives. As a therapeutic system, it strengthens trust in the unconditional meaningfulness of life and the dignity of the person. By applying this philosophy to the workplace, we can more deeply humanize our working lives and bring deeper meaning to work itself.

From the perspective of Logotherapy, we can find *unconditional meaning* in our work/life situations and experience the *unconditional value* of our colleagues as unique human beings. This is not an easy task but when we celebrate our differences as cheerfully as we celebrate our similarities the result is a powerful synergy at work *and* in the workplace. Bestselling author Stephen R. Covey, who has also been influenced by Frankl's teachings, has astutely observed that "difference is the beginning of synergy."[7] When business leaders and managers on all levels bring this awareness to work, they are the catalysts for profound changes in the workplace—changes that enhance everyone's ability to search for and find meaning, on the job, at home, and within our entire human experience.

> Unconditional meaning, however, is paralleled by the unconditional value of each and every person. It is that which warrants the indelible quality of the dignity of man. Just as life remains potentially meaningful under any conditions, even those which are most miserable, so too does the value of each and every person stay with him or her.[8]

Detecting Your Path

Of course, being fully human and living an authentic life at home, at play, and at work are formidable challenges at best. They involve a willingness to embark down a path of *self-discovery*, drawing heavily upon what Frankl refers to as our "will to meaning," that is, our inherent capacity to continually search for meaning under all circumstances. This human quest for meaning in every moment creates a discerning path that runs through all aspects of our lives. It is a path that weaves a process, not a product, for during our lifetime there is no final destination where everything comes to rest. This book offers guideposts along the way.

In Chapter 2, *Viktor Frankl's Lifework and Legacy*, we get a glimpse into the life and work of Dr. Frankl. As a mentor and author, he had a profound impact on my way of thinking and dramatically influenced my work and my life. As the founder of Logotherapy, he brought powerful insights and compassion to the therapeutic world, leaving a legacy of wisdom that only increases over time.

The many pathways to meaning are explored in Chapter 3, *Labyrinths of Meaning*, which also makes reference to the seven core principles of Frankl's work that were introduced earlier. Each of these life-meaning principles is then more deeply explored in individual chapters: *Exercise the Freedom to Choose Your Attitude* (Chapter 4); *Realize Your Will to Meaning* (Chapter 5); *Detect the Meaning of Life's Moments* (Chapter 6); *Don't Work Against Yourself* (Chapter 7); *Look at Yourself from a Distance* (Chapter 8); *Shift Your Focus of Attention* (Chapter 9); and *Extend Beyond Yourself* (Chapter 10).

> One may say that instincts are transmitted through the genes, and values are transmitted through traditions, but that meanings, being unique, are a matter of personal discovery.[9]

Chapter 4, *Exercise the Freedom to Choose Your Attitude*, examines the Logotherapeutic concept of *freedom of will*.

This concept is best described by Frankl's famous quote in *Man's Search for Meaning*, "Everything can be taken from a man but . . . the last of the human freedoms—to choose one's attitude in any given set of circumstances, to choose one's way."[10] The key ingredient here is the *responsibility* for choosing our attitude, which lies solely and soundly with the self.

Chapter 5, *Realize Your Will to Meaning*, explores Frankl's concept of our "will to meaning" and how we bring our values to life at work. Logotherapy, according to Frankl, "considers man as a being whose main concern consists of fulfilling a meaning and in actualizing *values*, rather than in the mere gratification and satisfaction of drives and instincts."[11] Giving meaning to work, in this context, means more than simply completing a task to receive a tangible reward, such as money, influence, status, or prestige. By committing to values and goals that might appear intangible but are nonetheless "real" and meaningful, we honor our deepest needs.

The fundamental presumption is that only as individuals can we answer for our own lives, detecting in them each moment's meaning and weaving our own unique tapestry of existence. Chapter 6, *Detect the Meaning of Life's Moments*, goes further—into the realm of ultimate meaning or "supermeaning." Frankl's holistic views on the importance of intuitive capacity for *love* and *conscience* offer great insight into how meaning at work and in everyday life reveals itself. Frankl has written: "Love is the ultimate and the highest goal to which man can aspire. . . . The salvation of man is through love and in love."[12] Yet our ability to weave love into our lives, especially into our work lives, is not only sadly limited but also suspect in today's "measurable" world of work.

Sometimes our most fervent desires and intentions are thwarted by our obsession with outcome. In Chapter 7, *Don't Work Against Yourself*, the technique known as "paradoxical intention" is examined and applied to work and everyday life. Frankl calls this form of self-sabotage "hyper-intention." The tendency to micro-manage the work of others, for example, may create hyper-intensive stress, performance anxiety, or even covert/overt actions of sabotage that can end up creating the opposite of the result sought by a manager. Sometimes focusing too closely on the problem can keep us from seeing the solution. Likewise, becoming obsessed with or fixated on a particular outcome, more often than not gets in the way of our best intentions.

Chapter 8, *Look at Yourself from a Distance*, focuses on the notion of self-detachment and how, among other things, it can help us to lighten up and not sweat the small stuff. Frankl observed that "Only man owns the capacity to detach himself from himself. To look at himself out of some perspective or distance."[13] This includes that uniquely human trait known as a sense of humor. Frankl noted that "no animal is capable of laughing, least of all laughing at *itself* or *about itself*."[14] A dose of self-detachment frees us to be more open and receptive about the universe of opportunities in our lives.

When Viktor Frankl was a prisoner in the Nazi concentration camps, in order to cope with stress, suffering, and conflict, he learned to deflect his attention away from the painful situation to other, more appealing circumstances. In Chapter 9, *Shift Your Focus of Attention*, we explore this skill and how it can be effectively used in the workplace.

Self-transcendence is explored in Chapter 10, *Extend Beyond Yourself*. This principle goes far beyond shifting the focus of attention from one thing to another. It takes us into the spiritual realm of ultimate meaning, where we see how our lives connect seamlessly to the lives of others. We see how being of service, no matter what the scale, is where our deepest meaning is realized.

Finally, in Chapter 11, *Living and Working with Meaning*, I weave my own views into Frankl's lessons so that they can be integrated into daily work/life, bringing personal and ultimate meaning to all the moments of our lives.

So, let's first take a look at Dr. Frankl's lifework, explore more fully the foundations of his meaning-centered approach, and see how we can apply his groundbreaking philosophy to work, workplace issues, and our personal lives.

Meaning Moment Recall a situation in which you felt especially *negative* about your job or career. Perhaps you just didn't like the work that you were doing, or maybe you disliked your supervisor, boss, or co-workers (this may even be your situation today). Did you view yourself as a "victim" of circumstances that were outside of your control, or did you feel responsible in some way for "creating" the situation and therefore were ultimately responsible for dealing with it? What, if anything, did you *do* about it? As you think about the situation now, what did you *learn* from it? What would you have done differently?

Life Doesn't Just Happen to Us

Meaning Question: What can _you_ do to make _your_ current work or job more meaningful?

FOR FURTHER
REFLECTION

Ask yourself honestly, are _you_ a "prisoner of your thoughts?" Do you hold _other_ people, including co-workers, "prisoners of your thoughts?"

2

Viktor Frankl's
Lifework and Legacy

I do not forget any good deed done to me,
and I carry no grudge for a bad one.[1]

It seems that I have known Viktor Frankl most of my life. It was in the late 1960s when I first became acquainted with his work and read his now-classic book, *Man's Search for Meaning*. While on active duty with the U.S. Army, I received formal training at Brooke Army Hospital in San Antonio, Texas, as a social work/psychology specialist. In addition to the opportunity to work side by side with some of the best mental health professionals in the field, this unique learning experience fueled my passion for studying various schools of thought and practice in psychiatry and psychology. Frankl's work, in particular, had great resonance for me at that time and eventually became an integral part of both my personal and professional life.

Over the years, in fact, I have had many opportunities to apply Frankl's teachings in my own life and work. In effect, I have been able to "field test" the validity and reliability of his key principles, often in comparison with competing schools of thought and in situations that tested the limits of my personal resiliency. Because it didn't take me long to realize the efficacy of his philosophy and approach, I became a *de facto* practitioner of Logotherapy long before the idea for this book surfaced in my mind.

I can recall many decisive times in my life, including situations that involved my work or employment, that could easily be described as turbulent and challenging. Such formidable, life-defining moments (although admittedly they often lasted much longer than a moment!) required a great deal of soul-searching for answers, and I remember how truly out of balance—and, yes, even lost—I felt at those critical times in my life. Parenthetically, I learned not many years ago from Thomas Moore, psychotherapist and author of the bestselling book *Care of the Soul,* that our most soulful times are when we are out of balance rather than when we are in balance! In any event, it was especially during these meaning-centered moments that I found myself putting Frankl's philosophy and approach to practice.

Let me now share a work-related example of when my personal resiliency was put to the test and how I applied some of Frankl's core principles to deal with the situation in a responsible manner. This life-defining situation involved my full-time, albeit summer, employment with a large engineering and construction firm in New Jersey. I had recently graduated from college and was contemplating going to law school after my military service. With the help and urging of my father, I took a job with the contract administration department at this company with the expectation that it would provide me with some useful legal experience and assist in my decision to pursue a career in law. My father, who was an engineer by profession, envisioned that some day I would work *for* him and his company as an attorney specializing in contract law.

This type of career path, I should note, was a far cry from what I had envisioned for myself, and the only interest that I had in law at the time was how it could be used as an instrument for social policy and societal change. To be sure, such a perspective, especially during the Vietnam War era, did not bode well for my relationship with my father and my employer. I didn't feature myself as a corporate attorney. I felt trapped and needed to resolve the situation quickly if, in my mind, I was going to survive the summer. Because I was keenly aware that working in the contracts administration department of this company was not the same thing as being a prisoner in a concentration camp, I began immediately to visualize and plan my escape route. Although my father had always been an authoritative figure in my life, I also realized that my situation, no matter how unbearable and confining it seemed to be, could never be compared to imprisonment in the Nazi death camps!

So, because of my familiarity with his work, I have Frankl to thank for helping me first assess my situation and then choose my response to it. First, I decided up front that I would maintain a *positive attitude* toward the situation, especially since I had an undeniable faith in my ability to orchestrate an eventual escape from my perceived predicament. Second, in no uncertain terms, the situation presented me with an opportunity to clarify and confirm my values toward the kind of work that I wanted to do, as well as *not* do. To use Frankl's words, I was determined to realize my *will to meaning* and only do work that was aligned with my core values.

Third, during the short time that I was employed by this company in New Jersey, I was able consciously to practice both the *de-reflection* and *self-detachment* principles of Logotherapy by shifting my focus of attention onto things that mattered to me and by maintaining a sense of humor, respectively. Fourth, my experience at the company and in my particular job assignment helped me to identify and weave together the various strands of meaning that seemed most important to me—both in terms of the kind of work that I wanted to do and the kind of life that I wanted to live. Even if it meant, which it did, standing up to and engaging in many heated arguments with my father so that I could declare the path that *I* wanted to pursue, I learned from this situation that it was worth the risk and effort!

In the end, my passion to realize my will to meaning translated into straining the relationship with my father, quitting my job, and changing my academic program objectives. In hindsight, however, the way that I chose to handle this particular situation—clearly a life-defining moment—also increased my personal resiliency for handling similar challenges in the future.

As you can gather, Frankl's thinking has profoundly influenced my life and work paths over the years. I've also had the great privilege of meeting Frankl personally and seeking his counsel. This book, in fact, is a product of Frankl's guiding influence and his personal encouragement.

A Life with Meaning

Viktor Frankl's calling came early. Long before the Holocaust took its horrific toll and became the ground from which sprang his most influential book, *Man's Search for Meaning*, Frankl's own search for meaning was already underway. At the tender age of 16, he gave his first public lecture, "On the Meaning of Life." Two years later, for his high school graduation essay, he wrote "On the Psychology of Philosophical Thought." It was almost as though on some level he was preparing for the tragedy that lay in his future and the role he would play in giving hope to all of humankind after the hopelessness and despair of the Holocaust. At a young age, Frankl had become convinced that the human spirit is what makes us unique and that reducing life and human nature to "nothing but," along the lines of many existentialist philosophers and psychiatrists of his time, denied or discounted any such spirit.

And it was not until he went through the hell of despair over the apparent meaninglessness of life, and struggled with the pessimism that was associated with such a reductionist and, ultimately, nihilistic or meaning-less view of life, that he was able to develop his therapeutic system of Logotherapy. At a conference in San Diego, in 1980, Frankl said that he had wrestled with this view that undercut faith in life's meaning, like Jacob with the angel did, until he could "say yes to life in spite of everything." Interestingly, an earlier version of *Man's Search for Meaning* had this very quotation as its title.

Frankl was born in Vienna, Austria, on March 26, 1905.

It was the day Beethoven died, and in his autobiography, he is quick to note this coincidence and reveal his sense of humor by sharing a comment made by one of his schoolmate's, "One mishap comes seldom alone."[2] His father, who had been forced to drop out of medical school for financial reasons, was a public servant who instilled in the young Viktor a spartan rationality along with a firm sense of social justice. For thirty-five years, Viktor's father had worked for the department of child protection and youth welfare. His mother, with whom he was very close, helped him develop his emotional side—the feelings and human connectedness that would inform his work as deeply as did his rationality and reasoning.

He was the second of three children and at an early age was afflicted with perfectionism. " . . . I do not even speak to myself for days," he said, referring to his anger at himself for not always being perfect. His astonishing and precocious interests led him to write to Sigmund Freud, with whom he had a correspondence throughout his high school years. It was a correspondence lost to Gestapo destruction years later, when Frankl was deported to the concentration camps.

In 1924, at Freud's request, Frankl published his first article in the *International Journal of Psychoanalysis*. He was 19 years old and had already developed two of his fundamental ideas: First, that we ourselves must answer the question that life asks *us* about the meaning of our lives, and that we ourselves are responsible for our existence. Second, that ultimate meaning is beyond our comprehension, and must remain so. It is something in which we must have faith as we pursue it. These ideas, established when he was a young man, were the basis for his observations during the years of his Nazi imprisonment. They survived the very darkest tests imaginable and, in fact, grew in strength for Frankl even as they were most challenged.

In 1924 he also started medical studies, and his growing professional recognition included a developing relationship with the renowned psychiatrist Alfred Adler. It was Adler who invited him to publish another article, this time in the *International Journal of Individual Psychology*. Frankl still was only 20 years old.

A year later, during public lectures in Germany, Frankl used the word *Logotherapy* for the first time. Frankl was not drawn to the dehumanizing nature of reductionism in psychotherapy. His work acknowledged human weakness but it went further to acknowledge the underlying meaning behind weakness and the potential we all have to learn from and transform our weaknesses. "I am convinced," he said, "that, in the final analysis, there is no situation that does not contain within it a seed of meaning."[3] This early belief of an idealistic young man became the foundation of Logotherapy, which continues today to inform and inspire our human struggle to search for and find meaning in our lives.

But, as in most scientific disciplines, it was not a simple, unchallenged path. By the time he received his medical degree in 1930, Frankl was banished from the Adler circle because he chose to support an alternative point of view. He had already gained an international reputation for his work in youth counseling, however, and from 1930 to 1938 was on the staff of the psychiatric University Clinic in Vienna. When in 1938 the Germans invaded Austria, he had an established private practice in neurology and psychiatry.

During the early part of the war, Frankl and his family were afforded a measure of protection because of his position as chief of the neurological department at Rothschild Hospital, the only Jewish hospital in Vienna. He risked his life and saved the lives of others by sabotaging, through the use of false diagnoses, the Nazi procedures requiring the euthanasia of mentally ill patients. It was during this time that he started writing his first book, *The Doctor and the Soul*, later to be confiscated by the Nazis.

In September 1942, Frankl and his family were arrested and deported to the Theresienstadt concentration camp near Prague. This was the beginning of three dark years of imprisonment during which Frankl lost his wife, Tilly, his parents, and his brother to the horrors of the Nazi prison camps. He was incarcerated at Auschwitz-Birkenau, Dachau, and finally, at Türkheim, where he nearly died from typhoid fever and kept himself going by reconstructing his manuscript on stolen bits of paper from the camp office. In his autobiography, Frankl recollected that, "I am convinced that I owe my survival, among other things, to my resolve to reconstruct that lost manuscript."[4]

In his book, *Man's Search for Meaning*, Frankl writes about his experiences in the concentration camps. He writes graphically and unflinchingly about the treatment, torture and murder of the prisoners. He also writes about the beauty of the human spirit; how it could transcend the horror and find meaning under the most unimaginable circumstances. Frankl's experiences and his observations served to reinforce the principles of meaning he had developed in his youth. At the end of the war, as a survivor and as a psychiatrist, he knew that his theories of Logotherapy had greater authenticity and ever deeper meaning. He wrote about the ongoing nightmares resulting from his experiences, but he also knew the same experiences laid the real groundwork for his belief in self-transcendence and the will to meaning.

> I can see beyond the misery of the situation to the potential for discovering a meaning behind it, and thus to turn an apparently meaningless suffering into a genuine human achievement. I am convinced that, in the final analysis, there is no situation that does not contain within it the seed of a meaning.[5]

After the war, Frankl returned to Vienna and became director of the Vienna Neurological Policlinic, a position he held for twenty-five years. He also started a long and distinguished academic career that took him to the University of Vienna, Harvard, as well as many other universities throughout the world. He received twenty-nine honorary doctorates during his life and wrote thirty-two books, which have been translated into twenty-seven languages. Man's Search for Meaning is considered to be one of the ten most influential books in America.

In 1992 the Viktor Frankl Institute was established in Vienna. Today, the institute continues to serve as the center of a worldwide network of research and training institutes and societies dedicated to advancing his philosophy and therapeutic system of Logotherapy and Existential Analysis. Frankl died peacefully on September 2, 1997, at the age of 92. He remained creative, productive, and passionate to the end of his life. His very presence touched and helped others. Indeed, psychologist Jeffrey Zeig, who was privileged to know Frankl and his family, anchored his sentiments about the influence of Frankl in words taken from Albert Camus's *The First Man*, "There are people who vindicate the world, who help others just by their presence." Without a doubt, Viktor Frankl was a man whose presence vindicated the world.

A Legacy of Meaning

The influence of Frankl's exceptional life and work has been profound. His writing alone has impacted people from all walks of life. Educators, students, religious leaders (including Roman Catholic Pope Paul VI), politicians, philosophers, psychologists, psychiatrists, and millions of others in search of meaning in their lives have been touched significantly by Frankl's work. Yet he was a humble man, modest and not interested in promoting himself in the fashion of the times.

He was also inspirational to those whose lives were anchored in struggle. For example, one young man from Texas, Jerry Long, age 17, was the victim of a paralyzing motor vehicle accident. He was left a quadriplegic and was able to type only by using a pencil-size rod that he held in his mouth. But he remained committed to becoming a psychologist because he liked people and wanted to help them. He wrote to Frankl after reading *Man's Search for Meaning*, remarking that his difficulties seemed to be far less than those suffered by Frankl and his comrades.

Yet Jerry found new insights every time he read Frankl's book. He said, "I have suffered but I know that, without the suffering, the growth I have achieved would not have been possible."

When he eventually met Dr. Frankl in person, he told him, "The accident broke my back, but it did not break me."[6]

In Frankl's words, "You do not have to suffer to learn. But, if you don't learn from suffering, over which you have no control, then your life becomes truly meaningless. . . . The way in which a man accepts his fate—those things beyond his control—can add a deeper meaning to his life. He controls how he responds."[7]

In the death camps of Nazi Germany, Frankl saw men who walked through the huts comforting others, giving away their last piece of bread. "They may have been few in number," he wrote, "but they offer sufficient proof that everything can be taken from a man but one thing: the last of human freedoms—to choose one's attitude in any given set of circumstances, to choose one's own way."[8]

This statement is perhaps one of the most often quoted references to Frankl's work. In this connection, U.S. Senator John McCain attributed his own survival as a prisoner of war in Vietnam for seven years in large part to the learning he acquired from Frankl's experience and teachings. In point of fact, Senator McCain began the preface to his book, *Faith of My Fathers* (1999), with this same Frankl quote.

In the realm of work and meaning, references to Frankl's work are numerous. Bestselling author, Stephen R. Covey, who wrote *The 7 Habits of Highly Effective People*, was particularly influenced by Frankl's vision. Referring to Frankl's concentration camp experience in *First Things First: To Live, to Love, to Learn, to Leave a Legacy*, Covey and his associates cited the following passage from *Man's Search for Meaning*: ". . . The single most important factor, he realized, was a sense of future vision—the impelling conviction of those who were to survive that they had a mission to perform, some important work left to do."[9]

Viktor Frankl, to be sure, leaves a profound legacy. Through his life and his work, he reminds us that we all have important work to do, that whatever we do is important, and that there is meaning everywhere, all the time.

 Meaning Moment Recall a situation at work in which you felt trapped or confined (this may even be your situation today). Perhaps you just didn't have the freedom or authority to deal with the situation in the way that, ideally, you would have liked. What, if anything, did you *do* about it? What, in other words, was your *escape* plan? As you think about the situation now, what did you *learn* from it? What would you have done differently?

 Meaning Question: What is *your* vision of the kind of work that you really *want* to do?

FOR FURTHER
REFLECTION

Consider the hardships that you have experienced in your own work life. How might Frankl's experience in the concentration camps help you deal with such hardships?

3

Labyrinths of Meaning

I wish to stress that the true meaning of life is
to be discovered in the world rather than within man
or his own psyche, as though it were a closed system.[1]

In an episode of the popular television comedy *Frasier* the central character, Dr. Frasier Crane, is notified that he will receive a Lifetime Achievement Award for his work as a psychiatrist and radio talk show host. Prior to the award ceremonies, Frasier seeks the counsel of his psychiatric mentor because he feels anxious and ambivalent about receiving the award. More fundamentally, however, the session with his mentor reveals that Frasier feels empty in spite of all his professional success. At the award ceremonies, his acceptance speech is noticeably brief and ends with the existential question, ". . . now what do I do with the *rest* of my life?" In this fictitious case, the concern is very real. Frasier had reached a critical point along his life path. And, like walking a labyrinth through all of its twists and turns, he couldn't see where he was going next.

A labyrinth is not a maze. It is not a puzzle to be solved but a path of meaning to be experienced. Its path is circular and convoluted but it has no dead ends. A labyrinth has one entrance, one way in and one way out. When we walk the path, we go around short curves and long curves; sometimes we are out on the edge, sometimes we circle around the center. We are never really lost, but we can never quite see where we are going. Along the path we sometimes move forward with ease and confidence; sometimes we creep ahead cautiously; sometimes we find the need to stop and reflect; and sometimes we even feel the urge to retreat. In so many ways, the labyrinth is like life. The center is there but our path takes us through countless twists and turns. Sometimes we are at the heart of our life experiences, sometimes we are at a playful turn; sometimes we share our path with others, sometimes we don't. No matter what, we are still *on* the labyrinth. It holds all our experience, in life and in work.

Many great cathedrals were built on the sites of ancient labyrinths. At Chartres Cathedral in France, the eleven-circuit labyrinth on the floor of the cathedral is considered by some as symbolic of the ancient pilgrimage to Jerusalem. But the labyrinth is also a metaphor for what is sacred in our lives. Through its twists and turns, its ancient spaciousness holds everything we experience—our minds and emotions, our physical beings and our spirits, our losses and our gains, our successes and our failures, our joys and our sorrows. When we walk the path inward, we carry our burdens with us. When we meditate or pray in the center, we ask for grace, forgiveness, and understanding. When we walk the path outward, we are lighter, more joyful, and ready yet again to take on our life's challenges.

Because of my Greek family heritage, I've long been fascinated with the Cretan labyrinth, a classical seven-circuit labyrinth dating back more than 4000 years. Some believe the Cretan design evolved from the spirals found throughout nature but it's the ancient myth of Theseus entering the labyrinth to fight the Minotaur that captured my imagination. As a child I wanted to explore the unknown; I wanted to be of service, even as I defied authority to find my way along the twists and turns of the path. And as convoluted as it sometimes was, the path has remained my own. As I reflect back, there is a harmony that I couldn't have predicted.

More than thirty years ago, I was introduced to the work of Viktor Frankl. Even though my work changed dramatically over the years, his teachings about meaning became the foundation of my working life. While serving on active duty with the U.S. Army in the late 1960s, I saw how the casualties of war—military and civilian—needed to find meaning in order to heal. In Chicago in the 1970s, while working in the mental health field, I saw how schizophrenics could find meaning and create meaningful lives without drugs, psychosurgery, or electroshock treatments. In the 1980s, I realized that linking the contradictions of business theory and practice was essential for an authentic life. In the 1990s, I began to understand that business could actually take the lead in societal and global transformation.

The labyrinth that is my life has taken me from the personal to the theoretical and back again. Yet, it is Frankl's deep belief in the inherent meaning of life that has steadily informed and inspired me, leading me deeper into my life path, deeper into authentic meaning.

When we explore our work lives as labyrinths of meaning, with all of the design features of classical labyrinths noted earlier, we deepen our experience. When we see our work as expressions of our bodies, minds, and spirits, we honor our inner lives as well as our connectedness to others and the outside world. Meaning is everywhere. This is true whether we drive a bus or run a corporation.

Not long ago, while attending a conference in New Orleans, I had the opportunity to encounter and experience Winston, a chartered bus driver for attendees of major conventions. To his customers, at least initially, Winston is only a bus driver, someone who makes sure that they travel between their hotel and the convention center safely and on time. To Winston, on the other hand, his customers represent a labyrinth of experience, as well as an important source of meaning at work and in his life.

"Welcome to Nawlins," Winston would say as he greeted everyone boarding his bus. In addition to pointing out what he felt were significant sights along his route, he would ask passengers if they had any questions about the city and was eager to offer *his* recommendations to enhance their personal experience. He would tell jokes and get everyone laughing, and was even able to engage all the passengers in a chant before the final stop: "Don't leave anything on the bus!" In short, Winston turned an ordinary bus ride into an extraordinary experience.

Not every conference attendee, you can imagine, was

open to or appreciative of his welcoming gestures, jokes, and counsel, preferring silence, especially in the early morning hours, to such exchanges during the bus ride. However, because Winston showed a genuine interest in learning about his customers—*who* they were, *where* they were from, *what* they did, *why* they were in town—he developed a rapport with them that was also truly *extra*ordinary. His engaging attitude, authenticity, and ability to connect with others added a dimension to the conference experience that was both memorable and meaningful.

In no uncertain terms, Winston showed that he truly cared about people, that he found meaning in his encounters with his customers, and that he was firmly committed to exploring his personal labyrinth—his inner bus route—through his work as a bus driver. In turn, Winston found deeper meaning in his work and therefore his work had deeper meaning to him and to those with whom he connected.

Any business leader or corporate CEO would be wise to follow Winston's lead. Yet in the corporate world it can be more difficult to find the daily moments of connection that nurture meaning. The bottom line is a harsh taskmaster. The levels of accountability in a business or corporation might not lend themselves to daily gratification. The opportunities to honor one another through moments of personal connection may be limited, yet the need is there. A business executive, like everyone else, needs to feel appreciated, understood, and fulfilled. The opportunities to feel connected "out there"—beyond the board room and office—have to be actively sought. And even when successful businesspeople already appreciate the link between their inner world and their business bottom line, it's not a simple weaving together of two ideals. Like the design of a labyrinth, it's a complex tapestry.

For Tom Chappell, President/CEO and co-founder, with his wife Kate, of Tom's of Maine, coming to terms with his business calling and his spiritual calling was a labyrinth of meaning that lasted more than thirty years. It took him on a personal journey through the most intimate parts of his inner life, even if it did start with clean clothes, safe soil, and toothpaste. Let me explain.

The 1960s and 1970s saw the beginning of the environmental movement. One of the first concerns was the chemical run-off that compromised the health of the soil and, ultimately, our groundwater systems, oceans, and lakes. In response to the times, Tom Chappell developed Clearlake, a non-phosphate liquid laundry detergent that was environmentally friendly in both product and packaging. Then it was Tom's of Maine toothpaste, an all-natural sugar-free product that was good for the body, that showed up in health-food stores. In those days, as a customer you had to go out of your way to find Tom's of Maine toothpaste; there was no natural foods section in the grocery store.

In many ways, it was a word-of-mouth awareness that established Tom's of Maine toothpaste; it symbolized a personal and ecological movement. (Why use sugar to clean your teeth if sugar causes cavities? Why hurt the environment if you don't have to?) Tom Chappell took his personal environmental ethic and applied it directly to his business—in both product and process. Since 1970, Tom's of Maine has flourished. The company has made its living, and its reputation, through its flagship toothpaste brand, as well as mouthwash, flossing ribbon, deodorants, soap, shampoo, shaving cream, decongestants, tonics, and herbal extracts made from natural ingredients and packaged in an environmentally friendly fashion—all now readily available at your local grocery store.

Thirty years, however, is a long time—people change—and so did Tom Chappell. In the mid-1980s, Tom faced a dilemma: he had to determine the direction and purpose of his company, and of his life. Would Tom's of Maine be a purely profit-based company or would he base the company's success on what he could actually achieve with the profits? And there was yet a more compelling, existential dilemma: was his company where he really belonged? Tom Chappell was feeling called by the Episcopal ministry and was considering leaving the company and going to the seminary.

His was a labyrinth of meaning that required heavy doses of ethical and personal decision making. His business had grown dramatically. The pressure to succeed at the bottom line, to grow profits above all, was reinforced by the MBA mentality of the new professionals who had joined his company. Some of them even wanted him to add saccharin to his toothpaste so it would be more palatable to the mainstream market. His original vision of commitment to natural products was facing compromise by the emphasis on company growth and profits. He no longer felt himself and his values being reflected by the company he had founded. Tom Chappell found his company less and less fulfilling. He began to search for inspiration elsewhere.

In 1988 he enrolled on a part-time basis at Harvard

Divinity School. For the next three years, Chappell spent two and a half days a week in Kennebunk, Maine, running the company, and the remainder of the work week going to school in Cambridge, Massachusetts. At Harvard, he studied the writings of the great moral and religious philosophers and tried to relate their ideas to business in general and to Tom's of Maine in particular.

Chappell was influenced by the work of Martin Buber, the twentieth-century Jewish philosopher who argued that we can have two opposite attitudes towards others, leading to two very different types of relationships. In the "I-It" relationship, we treat other people as objects and expect something back from each relationship. In the other, the "I-Thou" relationship, we relate to others out of respect, friendship, and love. In other words, we either see others as objects to use for our selfish purposes or we honor them for their own sake. Tom Chappell quickly recognized that he and Kate instinctively operated their company using the "I-Thou" relationship, but his professional managers were seeing it in terms of the "I-It" model.

Chappell was also deeply influenced by the writings of the eighteenth-century American philosopher, Jonathan Edwards. Edwards believed that an individual's identity comes not from being separate but from being connected or in relationship to others. Running with this notion, Chappell began thinking of Tom's of Maine in this light, perceiving it not simply as a private company but as a company in direct relationship to employees, customers, suppliers, financial partners, governments, the community, and even the earth itself.

Chappell's vision of his company as a social and moral entity, as well as a business organization, grew to more deeply reflect his spiritual beliefs, which in turn reinforced his connection to the outside world. His business continues to be a success in the broadest possible terms—satisfying his spiritual yearnings and will to meaning, as well as the bottom line. Tom's of Maine, founded on Chappell's youthful ideals, is now his mature ministry. Indeed, following the ideals of Viktor Frankl, it can be described as a ministry of meaning.

But meaning can be found at any given moment. Winston, the bus driver, effectively brings his spiritual self to life by seeing each bus-driving moment and passenger as an opportunity for compassion and connection. Even though his customers pass fleetingly through his life, he finds meaning through the experience of encountering others in his work. Tom Chappell, the unorthodox corporate executive, brings meaning to his multimillion dollar business through sustained connection to—and creative expression with—his employees, his customers, his products, and the planet.

In the workplace, we can either choose actively to look for and find meaning or we can see our jobs as something outside our "real" lives. If we choose the latter, we cheat ourselves out of an enormous amount of life experience. Even if we think we hate our jobs, by stopping long enough to connect, inside *and* out, to our broader relationship to meaning, we can find rewards. The question, of course, is do we want to make such a meaning-full connection? What if we don't have the personal drive of a Tom Chappell or the human compassion of a Winston? What if we are in mundane jobs that are repetitive and boring?

Our first task is to stop complaining. If we are honest, we know how happy it can make us to find something to complain about at work. It's even more fun if we really do have something, or someone, to complain about. We often make meaning by complaining. This can feel momentarily satisfying, but ultimately it undermines the integrity of our experience. It takes the meaning out of our work and out of our relationship to our work. This doesn't mean it's not necessary to complain once in awhile, perhaps even to whine and groan about the job. What it means is that we need to be *aware* of when and why we are complaining. Is it to bring about a simple moment of relief? Or, have we started to define our work by habitually negative perceptions?

All of us know people who, as creatures of habit, define their work or job in this negative way, don't we? As a case in point, let's take Bob, who for years has worked in the financial services industry. In fact, Bob has had many moments of apparent career "success," having attained key executive positions in several banks, including that of president. Bob's labyrinth of meaning at work, however, has taken him through some dramatic twists and turns, and he rarely if ever seems positive or optimistic about his circumstances on the job and, by implication, in his life. As a consequence, Bob complains incessantly about his responsibilities, his colleagues, his customers, his community, and about every other aspect of his working life. And if we were to discuss his experiences walking the labyrinth of meaning at work—that is, along his career path—we would hear nothing but stories of misery, negativity, and despair. Unlike Victor Hugo's character, Jean Valjean in *Les Misérables*, Bob to this day seems unable (or unwilling) to fulfill his meaning potential, due in large part to his negative, always complaining, posture toward his work.

Complaining about our miserable jobs around the water cooler, or starting a "bitch and moan club" at the office, might offer a moment of camaraderie but it doesn't nurture meaning, for us or for others. The idea that work is neither fun nor fulfilling, nor should it be, takes a huge toll on our ability to bring meaning to our work. When we make complaining a habit, we make meaninglessness a habit. Before long, we are invested in our complaining so deeply that all opportunity to see our work experience as a rich part of our lives vanishes. Instead of taking the time to find meaning, we take the time to find and focus on *meaninglessness*. So, from now on, ask yourself why you complain and, perhaps more important, what's the payoff from your complaining.

Remember also that the great complaint carnival is not a celebration; it's a bandwagon of misery. Our complaints trivialize our experience—both at work and in our personal lives. When we complain, we disconnect. When we complain, we hold whatever or whoever we're complaining about as a shield between us. We perpetuate an old community of victimization and helplessness. But when we take the time to communicate about our fears and insecurities, our real lives, we connect on a deeper, authentic level. When we connect through this deeper humanness, we create a new community of support and possibility. It's a support that can nurture far beyond the realm of the water cooler.

When we stop long enough to make this kind of

authentic connection, we can't avoid meaning. It's waiting for us around every water cooler, in every elevator, every cubbyhole, taxi cab, conference room, and corporate board room. When we miss the meaning in our work life, we miss the life in our work. And when we miss the life in our work, we can't help but become a prisoner of our thoughts—confined within our own inner concentration camp.

Viktor Frankl excavated the darkest of despair and discovered meaning. He didn't have to create it; it was there waiting to be found. So it is in our work lives. When we open ourselves to meaning, when we stop long enough to appreciate ourselves, and others, at work in meaningful ways, we immediately enhance the quality of our own lives as well as the lives of those around us.

This does not mean that we deny our burdens, our grief, and our worries and sign on to some Pollyanna perspective of the world. On the contrary. Frankl knew well through his experience in the Nazi concentration camps the meaning of unavoidable suffering. He also knew the very darkest of human behavior and the brightest light of human possibility—at the same time. He carried the awareness of both potentialities, and this awareness deepened his humanity and created in him a deep and abiding faith. He saw people rise out of the most depraved circumstances and offer all they had to others. He saw the manifestation of spirit on a daily, minute-to-minute basis.

To be sure, we all know generosity and grace, those moments when someone says or does just the right thing, offers us the presence we need to see things more clearly, to feel comforted in a difficult time. So why, when so much of our lives happens at work, can't such attention to one another also have a place?

Our lives present us with a labyrinth of meaning, and so do our jobs. And it's not always evident. Life and relationships unfold; they change; we change; sometimes we embrace the process; sometimes we change our circumstances and start over. This is true in work as well as in our private lives. Again, it is part of the labyrinth of our life. We are on one path and it takes us through many turns of fate and fortune, pain and pleasure, loss and gain. It is a path that shapes us, that uncovers our fears, that tests our courage, and that leads us to this very moment. It is a sacred path of individuality and no one walks it but us.

It is not an easy task to stay the course with reverence while walking the labyrinth. But no matter what our faith persuasion is, or whether we even have one, honoring our own path is essential if we are to know authentic meaning in our lives. And only when we know meaning in our lives can we know meaning in our work. *Our will to meaning, not our will to pleasure or our will to power, is what illuminates our lives with true freedom.* This is an extremely important distinction to make as we explore the ways in which we bring our will to bear on our lives and in our work. In the final analysis, we are free to choose *our* responses to everything that happens in our lives, including those things that happen through our work. This strikes at the very heart of Frankl's teachings and is the basis of the core principle to be explored in the next chapter.

Meaning Moment Recall a situation in your work life in which you were faced with a major decision to shift direction (this may even be your situation today). Perhaps you were faced with a boss or co-worker who was challenging your style or method of doing your job. Or, perhaps you found yourself in some kind of ethical dilemma or value conflict that pressured you to change direction in some way. What, if anything, did you actually *do* about it? As you think about the situation now, what did you *learn* from it? What would you have done differently?

? **Meaning Question: How do *you* deal with negativity and habitual complaining in the workplace?**

FOR FURTHER
REFLECTION

How might the labyrinth metaphor help *you* find greater meaning and fulfillment at work? Think about how you might use this metaphor in a constructive way with your colleagues or co-workers.

(**4**)

Exercise the Freedom to Choose Your Attitude

Everything can be taken from a man but . . .
the last of the human freedoms—to choose one's attitude
in any given set of circumstances, to choose one's way.[1]

It was nearly midnight. It was time to jot down his final thoughts before darkness fell around him. In just a few minutes, the lights would go out and his cell would no longer be a "writer's study"; it would be a stark, confining dungeon. For almost twenty years, this had been his home, his office, and his prison. But even though he knew it was not likely that he would ever see real freedom again, he remained true to his core values and life goals. He wrote several book-length manuscripts, stayed in touch with his loved ones, and persevered with optimism. His defiant human spirit prevailed.

With a great deal of pride, I can tell you that he is my great-uncle, General Stylianos Pattakos, a Greek patriot who served his country as a military officer and political leader through some of the most turbulent times in modern Greek history. Among other things, my uncle Stelios was one of three officers responsible for setting up a military regime in Greece in 1967. He served in various ways, including as the country's vice president, until another government takeover in 1974.

It was because of his role in the so-called Greek junta that Uncle Stelios was charged with the crime of treason and imprisoned. Thankfully, there was enough support for him as a person and as a Greek patriot that eventually his role in history was reconsidered and his life spared. In 1995, he was released and was finally able to share his story.

Like the renowned Viktor Frankl, Nelson Mandela, U.S. Senator John McCain, and Burma's Aung Sang Suu Chi—along with unknown numbers of other courageous and imprisoned people—Uncle Stelios was challenged to understand the deeper meaning of "freedom" even as he dealt with the loss of personal liberties and human dignity. In other words, despite his physical incarceration, my uncle Stelios was called upon to rely on his *will to meaning* in order to gain a different kind of freedom—one that distinctly came from within himself—so that he could survive his long ordeal in prison.

There is a story involving Nelson Mandela that also serves to illuminate the relationship between personal freedom and imprisonment. The day that Mandela was being released from prison on Robben Island, Bill Clinton, then Governor of Arkansas, was watching the news. He quickly called his wife and daughter and said, "You must see this, it is historical." As Mandela stepped out, Clinton saw a flush of anger on his face as he looked at the people watching; then it disappeared.

Later, when Clinton was president of the United States and Mandela was president of South Africa, the two leaders met and Clinton told about his observation during Mandela's release from prison. And, because Mandela had always been a model of reconciliation with no spirit of revenge or negativism, President Clinton candidly asked him for an explanation of what seemed to have occurred on that historic day. President Mandela replied, "Yes, you are right. When I was in prison, the son of a guard started a Bible Study and I attended; . . . and that day when I stepped out of prison and looked at the people observing, a flush of anger hit me with the thought that they had robbed me of twenty-seven years. Then the Spirit of Jesus said to me, 'Nelson, while you were in prison you were free, now that you are free, don't become their prisoner.'"[2]

It's neither proper nor possible to compare the ways in which each of these people endured unthinkable experiences. But in their very presence in our lives, they represent real people who experienced real suffering; and each, in his or her own way, triumphed. These people were compelled, each under uniquely dreadful circumstances, to find meaning within their imprisoned lives. Stripped of most of the freedoms that we take for granted, as prisoners they were left with what Frankl called the "last of the human freedoms"— the freedom to choose their attitude in response to their life circumstances.

This freedom to choose is ours in every aspect of our lives. Yet it can be difficult, even when our lives are comparably safe and perceivably "free." In some way, we all struggle with things beyond our control. Bringing them under our control, even if only in an attitudinal sense, is where our freedom takes shape, no matter what the circumstances.

Christopher Reeve had it all. In addition to his early success on Broadway, he was known all over the world for his leading role in *Superman*, the movie that made him a star. At the age of 42 years, his acting career was bright and his life was filled with unlimited possibilities. Indeed, he was passionate about life on all levels and was intent on experiencing it with gusto. An all-around athlete, Reeve loved sailing and was a skilled equestrian, skier, ice skater, and tennis player.

On Memorial Day of 1995, however, the world held its breath as Christopher Reeve struggled for life. Reeve had been thrown from his horse in an accident that broke his neck and left him unable to move or breathe. The man who was Superman had become a quadriplegic. But, as he wrote in his bestselling autobiography, appropriately entitled *Still Me*, "I think a hero is an ordinary individual who finds strength to persevere and endure in spite of overwhelming obstacles."[3] And so continues the story of the real Superman.

In the years since the accident, Reeve has not only survived, but thrived—fighting for himself, for his family, and for thousands of people with spinal cord injuries in the United States and around the world. An inspirational force, Reeve displayed his choice to maintain a positive attitude toward his situation on *Larry King Live*, just ten months after his accident: "I am a very lucky guy," he said. "I can testify before Congress. I can raise funds. I can raise awareness."[4]

Importantly, Christopher Reeve has credited his wife Dana and his three children for quickly lifting him out of an initial morass of hopelessness. "You learn the stuff of your life (sports, movies) . . . that's not the essence of your existence," he said. "My relationships were always good. Now they have transcended. That's why I can honestly say I am a lucky man," he said. He goes further:

> When a catastrophe happens, it's easy to feel so sorry for yourself that you can't see anybody around you. But the way out is through your *relationships* [emphasis added]. The way out of that misery or obsession is to focus more on what your little boy needs or what your teenagers need or what other people around you need. It's very hard to do, and often you have to force yourself. But that is the answer to the dilemma of being frozen—at least it's the answer I found."[5]

As we see in Christopher Reeve's case, it was the fact that he exercised his freedom to choose his attitude about his life and work that enabled him to take the bold steps of confronting the unforeseen changes in his life path. In so doing, he was able to do more than simply cope with his personal suffering and loss. By exercising his freedom to choose, Reeve unleashed his potential for self-healing and discovered a path to authentic meaning that may have gone unnoticed. As a byproduct of his conscious choice, he also was able to remind us that life is not to be taken for granted, but to be lived fully with passion, curiosity, and gratitude.[6]

In life's most difficult situations, it is our capacity to cope and personal resiliency that are put to the ultimate test. It's then that the freedom to choose our attitude takes center stage. To exercise this freedom effectively, however, we must be able to view any given situation from different vantage points. We must know who we are and be flexible and courageous enough to make a shift when necessary, even if it means moving away from what is expected or considered "normal."

The responsibility for choosing our attitude lies solely and soundly with each one of us. It cannot be transferred to someone else. I have made this claim over the years to various corporate and government clients, especially in cases where workers, including executives and managers, seem intent on "bitching and moaning" about their working conditions but don't appear willing to do anything about them. I'm reminded of the *Far Side* cartoon that shows people mingling at a "Part of the Problem" Convention because it illustrates to an absurd level how limited and negative our thinking can become. We celebrate our freedom to choose our attitude at work only when we decide to move from being a part of the problem to becoming a part of the solution.

And in our personal lives, too, it doesn't work to wait for solutions magically to arrive; we have to be a part of the solution. NBA coach Phil Jackson, in his book *Sacred Hoops,* cautions us to remember that the best way to realize your dreams is to wake up! In other words, being part of any solution means taking action.

Through our life experiences and the investment that we make in personal growth and development, our repertoire of coping skills can and usually does change over time. We invest in ourselves—through such things as training or counseling—and the return on this investment is a renewed effectiveness in dealing with life's situations.

Unless there was a 100% guarantee that I will be killed here on the spot, and I will never survive this concentration camp last part of my life, unless there is any guarantee, I'm responsible for living from now on in a way that I may make use of the slightest chance of survival, ignoring the great danger surrounding me in also all the following camps I had been sent. This, as it were, a coping, not mechanism, but a coping maxim I adopted, I espoused, at that moment.[7]

In Frankl's case, had he not adopted his coping beliefs upon his arrival at Auschwitz, he might not have been able to sustain his optimistic and passionate view about his chances of survival. By choosing his fundamental attitude, which he called his "coping maxim," the coping mechanisms in his psychiatrist tool kit then became more meaningful and effective. His decision to experience meaning under desperate circumstances enabled him to act on his own behalf as well as on behalf of others.

What lessons can we learn from Frankl's experience? Think about difficult situations in your life or work in which your attitude played a defining role in how well you were able to cope. Think about the coping mechanisms that were at your disposal. Did you choose to use them? Why or why not? How effective were you in coping with the situation? Now ask yourself a more fundamental question: What guides your coping skills? What principle or principles underlie your decision making in complex and challenging situations? It can be difficult to articulate these deeper ideals and values in our lives. If nothing definitive comes immediately to mind, jot down your initial thoughts on this question for later use in framing a more complete answer.

Ponder also the times when you observed people who

were guided by their coping skills in difficult decision-making situations. I am sure you can identify cases of extraordinary resolve by your co-workers, family members, and friends during times of hardship—personal or professional. Although these situations may not have been as catastrophic as that experienced by Viktor Frankl, they may still have been formidable challenges to overcome or survive.

In the workplace, it is clear that some individuals are able to cope more easily than others with the outpouring of professional changes in today's job market. Corporate downsizing, mergers and acquisitions, new technologies, career or job shifts, and the trauma of unemployment are all part of our work lives. All of us can tell stories that illustrate the many ways in which people respond to these challenges. In the final analysis, the most capable, responsible, and resilient individuals have adopted, consciously or unconsciously, a coping maxim and skills to guide and drive them towards meaningful resolution.

When we choose our attitude in light of what I would call *true optimism*, we actually make three choices: (1) we choose a positive attitude about the situation at hand; (2) we choose an attitude that supports a form of creative visualization about what's possible; and (3) we choose an attitude that generates passion for the action that makes the possible become a reality. In other words, being a true optimist actually requires more than positive thinking. Positive affirmations, like good intentions, aren't enough; we need to be able to *visualize* the possibilities that may result from our choice of attitude, and be able to feel the emotion or *passion* behind our choice of attitude that will help us actualize such possibilities. We each have the freedom to make these choices, but it is amazing how frequently we don't. We either "choose" to abstain from taking full responsibility for what should be our conscious choices or "choose," albeit unconsciously, to remain frozen in thought patterns that may no longer serve our highest good. In short, we become a *prisoner of our thoughts*.

In my work, I have encountered clients, co-workers, friends, and family members who are stuck in old habits of self-imprisonment. They display the "power of negative thinking" about a given work or life situation, assuring that they could never visualize a better tomorrow. Or they are steeped in so much fear of the unknown that they have essentially immobilized themselves, effectively avoiding any kind of risk. The ultimate freedom to choose their attitude and their future, no matter how desperate they may be, seems as foreign to them as a life in which they could feel truly fulfilled and happy.

In the workplace, I have seen many instances in which organizational change has resulted in people losing their jobs. In one particular case, I had a friend, Tom, who had been let go by a high-tech firm after many years of faithful service. Although Tom clearly did not agree with the company's decision to release him, and he felt that his value was neither acknowledged nor fully understood, he realized that he was given no choice but to move on with his life.

Ironically, Tom had discussed leaving the company many times in the past, but could not bring himself to make the decision to leave on his own. And while he felt positive about his chances for a new position or new work, he was unable to visualize the possibilities. He even shared with me that he could not see himself doing something else. When the company's decision to release him finally became a reality, he was forced to change his attitude.

"For the most part," he said, "My mind is racing 1,000 miles an hour—which, in itself, is absolutely great. Maybe uncertainty brings out the best in us."

Forced to take a leap, Tom, by changing his attitude about his freedom, was able to change his attitude about his future. He is now combining several opportunities that more deeply reflect his passion, values, and interests. Ironically, it took the company's decision to let him go before he was able to see the possibility of realizing his meaning potential, his will to meaning.

To show that it is never too late, let me share another example of how the freedom to choose your attitude can be exercised in a work-related situation. One of my good friends and colleagues is a creativity consultant in her late eighties. Like Viktor Frankl, Rebecca is yet another source of insight and inspiration, especially for those a lot younger who are facing changing circumstances. Rebecca, due to a severe hip injury, had to be confined to a wheelchair, which severely restricted her ability to move around, travel, and generally live her active life. Not to be dismayed, she remained positive about her plight; she visualized a redesigned work situation for herself and took action to bring it about—all at the age of 89 years young! Rebecca still consults with individuals and organizations, but with a renewed focus on disabled workers. More than simply positive thinking, hers is a case of true optimism. She exercised her freedom to choose her attitude under difficult circumstances and expanded her life creatively in yet a new way.

We all have this ultimate freedom but, again, each of us must make an active choice to exercise it. The first questions to ask yourself when facing a challenging situation are: Are you aware of your current attitude toward the situation? Are you willing to change it? This is a subtle process because often we may be unaware of our attitude toward something (or someone) and/or we may not really want to address the possibility of changing our attitude, let alone be willing to do so. With this in mind, here is a quick exercise that can help you address such issues, not only by opening up new possibilities but also by helping you to exercise your freedom to choose your attitude.

To begin with, think of a situation at work or in your personal life that is or was especially stressful, negative, or challenging for you. Now, take a deep breath, and write down *ten positive things* that could result—or did result—from this situation. Notice any resistance you may have to doing this. (Sometimes it's easier to stay mad, or self-righteous, or right.) But just let your mind loose and entertain the possibilities. Write down what first comes to mind. Continue to stretch your imagination and suspend judgment, listing whatever comes into your consciousness, no matter how silly, far out, or unrealistic your thoughts may appear to be. Feel completely free to determine or define what "positive" means to you.

After you have completed your list, look at it closely, and let the positive become possible in your frame of reference regarding the difficult situation. Sometimes this is very hard to do. It requires a letting go of old ways of thinking, pain, remorse, disappointment, frustration, perhaps even grief and anguish. But it levels your playing field of possibilities for the future. Experience has shown that this exercise opens you to deep optimism no matter how challenging your circumstances.

The first time I was introduced to this exercise, I was given the following instruction: "List Ten Positive Things If You Died Today." I was unaccustomed to discussing, let alone exploring, the possibilities of my death, and thought the exercise totally absurd. It turned out to be quite the opposite. In fact, the participants at my session, including Yours Truly, had a great deal of fun with this exercise once we allowed ourselves the freedom to let go. Most of us were eventually able to see the silver lining in something even as catastrophic as our death. Our group energy increased dramatically, and we all had opportunities to learn new things about ourselves, each other, and the often-taboo topic of death. I have since used this exercise with hundreds of client groups with similar success.

Now, if we can find something positive to say about our own death, it should be easy to find something positive to say about our work situation, family life, and so forth, don't you think? My experience over many years is that no matter how catastrophic the event, whether work-related or personal, eventually there is *always* something positive that results from it.

Let me share a personal experience that may help to clarify what I mean. Years ago, while still a full-time professor, I was driving to campus early one morning to teach a class. It was a very peaceful morning, there was no traffic, and I was enjoying the solitude as I listened to relaxing music on the radio. I remember driving down a tree-lined street, with a grass island in center, that had cars parked tightly on both sides. And, coming up the street toward me was a school bus van, the only other moving vehicle in sight. All of a sudden, for no apparent reason, I saw the van veer out of control and crash into one of the parked cars on its side of the street. I couldn't believe it! Immediately, I stopped my car and rushed over to the van to see what I could do.

The front of the van was crushed and I could see and smell smoke. While I prayed that someone in the neighborhood had heard the crash and called 911, I pulled the driver, a young woman, out of the vehicle and, as carefully as I could, carried her to a nearby lawn. I could tell she was injured and, even more, upset by what had happened. She began to cry as she said, "Oh no, what am I going to do? I just got this job; my parents are going to kill me!"

Still waiting for someone, preferably an ambulance, to arrive and help with the situation, I was at a loss for what to do at that particular moment. I wanted to keep the young lady as calm as possible. Without really thinking about the consequences, I looked her straight in the eyes and said: "Let's list *ten positive things* about this accident." I started with: (1) there were no children in the school van; (2) there was nobody in the parked car that was struck; (3) neither vehicle had exploded or was on fire (at least not at that point); (4) somebody was around to help her in her moment of need; and (5) she's still alive and conscious. You get the picture. In any event, by the time we identified only a few of the items on this list of positives about the accident, the driver actually began to smile! And, importantly, when the ambulance finally arrived, and I explained to the emergency medical technician what we had done while waiting, he said that her shift in attitude had most likely prevented her from going into shock.

A key lesson to be learned from this experience? Even if you don't see the cognitive or emotional benefits of maintaining a positive attitude toward a situation you are facing, be it at work or in your personal life, please consider the physiological benefits. One of the real powers of positive thinking is that it is good for your health!

From the perspective of work, here now are some questions that have been posed in a number of settings:

- "List ten positive things that would happen if you lost your job today."

- "List ten positive things that would happen if your department was eliminated today."

- "List ten positive things that would happen from a breakdown in a production line."

- "List ten positive things that would happen if the work week was changed from 5-days/8-hours per day to 4-days/10-hours per day."

- "List ten positive things that would happen from a 20% budget cut."

In all of these situations there were benefits, both in terms of process and product outcomes. First of all, everyone involved acknowledged that they were free to choose their attitude and view their situation from many different perspectives; second, no matter how desperate the situation or condition confronted, everyone acknowledged that something positive could result, even in the situations that seemed ridiculous at first. Also, in responding to these questions, the positive energy among individuals, especially in work groups or teams, increased dramatically. The varied opportunities to view the situation or condition in a new light increased, as did the opportunities to resolve the challenges. Through this exercise, the participants learned an effective way to release themselves, at least partly, from their self-imposed thought prisons.

Before moving on, let me share with you a unique application of the "Ten Positive Things" exercise in the workplace. The situation involved a client training session that I was conducting in Alaska with the U.S. Forest Service. At the end of the first day of a two-day session, I overheard comments from one of the more macho male participants, Paul, that he was not at all interested in the training and didn't feel that it was relevant to him. The Ten Positive Things exercise had been introduced and practiced that afternoon and Paul was not impressed.

The next morning, when I returned to the training venue, I noticed Paul sitting beside two female participants, laughing and giggling. When I asked him what had happened, he reported that when he went home the evening after our session, he was shocked to learn that his teenage daughter had received a tongue piercing and was now sporting a new piece of jewelry in her mouth! Angry and upset,

Paul argued with his daughter and wife; in short, he had a terrible night with his family. When he returned to the training session the next day, looking tired and depressed, he confessed to his two female co-workers what had happened. Immediately, they asked him to list the Ten Positive Things from his daughter's tongue piercing! Working together, they not only came up with many potential positives to be gained from his stressful experience, but also fostered an entirely new (and positive) attitude toward his daughter *and* the training session! Indeed, things could have been worse for his teenage daughter—doing this exercise put this situation in perspective for Paul and ultimately helped him change his attitude about it.

> As a human phenomenon, however, freedom is all too human. Human freedom is finite freedom. Man is not free from conditions. But he is free to take a stand in regard to them. The conditions do not completely condition him. Within limits it is up to him whether or not he succumbs and surrenders to the conditions. He may as well rise above them and by so doing open up and enter the human dimension . . . Ultimately, man is not subject to the conditions that confront him; rather, these conditions are subject to his decision. Wittingly or unwittingly, he decides whether he will face up or give in, whether or not he will let himself be determined by the conditions.[8]

In our lives we have courageous role models to learn from as we explore the vast reaches of our own freedom. Many are public heroes, honored by history or celebrity status. Others are to be found in our friends, in our families, and in our communities. My own Uncle Stelios, through his choices, his attitudes, and his commitment to his own values and future, embodies for me the many facets of Viktor Frankl's meaning-centered philosophy. Although we may not be totally free from the various conditions or situations that confront us—in our personal and work lives—the important thing is that we can choose how we respond, at the very least through our choice of attitude. According to Frankl, this is not only our right as full human beings; it is our full human beingness to be free. All we have to do is resist the temptation of remaining a "prisoner of our thoughts" and choose this freedom, no matter what.

 Meaning Moment   Recall a situation in your work life in which you consciously exercised the freedom to choose your attitude about it (this may even be your situation today). Perhaps you were faced with a difficult boss or co-worker. Or, perhaps you were confronted by a change in job. What was your attitude at first toward the situation? How did it change? What, if anything, did you actually *do* about changing your attitude? As you think about the situation now, what did you *learn* from it? What would you have done differently?

 Meaning Question: How do *you* maintain a *positive attitude* at work or in the workplace?

FOR FURTHER
REFLECTION

How might Frankl's notion of a "coping maxim" (an overall belief about coping) help *you* find greater meaning and fulfillment at work? Think also about how you might use this technique in a positive and constructive way with your colleagues or co-workers.

Realize Your Will to Meaning

A man who becomes conscious of the responsibility he bears toward a human being who affectionately waits for him, or to an unfinished work, will never be able to throw away his life. He knows the "why" for his existence, and will be able to bear almost any "how".[1]

"It's going to be a fun week, sailing the Endeavor, tennis, golf, eating, drinking. All the things we are best known for," said former Tyco CEO Dennis Kozlowski. This statement was recorded on a videotape of a $2 million birthday bash that Kozlowski threw for his wife on the island of Sardinia in 2000. An edited version of the tape was shown to jurors in Kozlowski's larceny trial, and it provided further evidence that Tyco had funded its ex-CEO's lavish lifestyle for years before he resigned in June 2002. Alas, Sigmund Freud would be proud, for Dennis Kozlowski demonstrated that his theory of the Pleasure Principle, also known as the *will to pleasure*, is alive and well in corporate America!

Tyco, of course, is not the only major company in recent times that has faced public scrutiny, as well as the wrath of government regulators and the courts, due to corporate scandals. Nor is Kozlowski the only (ex)CEO to have gained such notoriety. Do the names, Ken Lay (Enron), Bernie Ebbers (Worldcom), and Martha Stewart ring a bell? Interestingly, there are websites dedicated to profiling such infamous individuals, even on playing cards, and highlighting the most notorious of the corporate scandals in which they were involved.[2] Many of these executives, it should be noted, did not appear as interested in following Freud's will to pleasure as they were in pursuing Alfred Adler's *will to power* (in Adler's words, "striving for superiority"). Adler, you may remember, was a contemporary (and, to a degree, a mentor) of Viktor Frankl.

To Frankl, however, both Freud's will to pleasure and Adler's will to power were manifestations of something missing, which hinted that there was yet another explanation for the kinds of behaviors exhibited by the former corporate icons identified here. In effect, the need or drive to seek pleasure à la Freud and the relentless pursuit of power à la Adler were really just attempts to cover up, but not necessarily fill, a void of *meaning* that existed in the lives of these individuals. Put differently, because their will to meaning had been frustrated, for whatever reasons, they chose alternative paths to follow—paths based on the premise that pleasure and/or power would somehow be able to replace what had been missing.

Only the search for meaning, Frankl would say, holds the potential to bring the kind of authentic enrichment and fulfillment that most people desire from their work and in their everyday lives. And it is the ability to realize our *will to meaning*—our authentic commitment to meaningful values and goals that only we can actualize and fulfill—that guides us in the quest to tap into this distinctly *human* potential. Unlike either Freud or Adler, Frankl considers the main concern of human beings to be fulfilling a meaning and actualizing values, rather than simply the gratification and satisfaction of drives and instincts.

We've already seen examples of people, including corporate executives, who clearly demonstrate the central importance of Frankl's will to meaning in their work lives. And while such individuals may also want (or seek) pleasure and authority, the primary motivation for their existence is not pleasure or authority. So, when Bill Hewlett and David Packard, for example, built their company, Hewlett-Packard, from a one-car garage into one of the world's most admired success stories, it was a particular set of *meaningful values*, known as "The HP Way," that guided them in identifying and meeting their objectives, in working with one another, and in dealing with customers, shareholders, and others.[3]

It is important to acknowledge that not all values are created equal. Actualizing values like those exclusively associated with pleasure and power would not, in Frankl's mind, constitute the way to fulfill authentic meaning. Against this backdrop, let me share a statement made to me by a government employee, who referred to values as the "things that make life worth living." In other words, by relying on our moral compass, or what psychologist and author James Hillman refers to as our "Soul's Code," we may uncover values that are truly meaningful and worth pursuing in our work and everyday lives. As we shall see in this chapter, a personal (and organizational) commitment to such positive, life-affirming values is clearly a manifestation of Frankl's will to meaning!

How many of us have looked forward to a beautifully planned holiday and then felt disappointed after it was over? How often does the promise of pleasure captivate us, only to leave us unsatisfied after the event happens, no matter how perfect it seemed at the time? This is true with everything from drugs and sex to pay raises and vacations. It's the *promise* of pleasure that we are lured by; pleasure itself is fleeting. We come down with a cold on the plane to paradise. We get a sad phone call from a family member that dashes plans for a romantic evening. Our teenage daughter puts a dent in the new car and it's no longer perfect. We feel excited about what we purchased during a shopping spree, only to find the thrill gone after only a week. Moments of *true* pleasure come to us when we aren't looking for them. They are gifts uncalled for, moments that transcend our planning, moments that transcend even our perception of pleasure.

The search for power in our lives is parallel to our search for pleasure. It is "out there." Power over our employees, our bosses, our customers, our shareholders, our kids, the waitress in a restaurant, or a clerk in a retail store is illusory at best and terribly destructive at worst. We think we might have power but we never know for sure. Even if we do, in the power game there's always an opponent, the ground is always shifting. Much like Sisyphus, the Greek hero who was ordered by the gods to push a big rock uphill only to see it slip out of his hands in the last moment, our search for power becomes an endless—and joyless—undertaking.

A few decades ago, when group therapy took center stage in the self-awareness movement, one exercise in particular illuminated the power principle. A group was asked to spend some time together and choose a leader. After they had carefully selected a leader, the group was then asked to go back and select the person most responsible for choosing the leader. It was the leader behind the leader who was the real leader. When power is the playground, there's always another power waiting in the wings. Power is an exhausting game to play and, like pleasure, power is fleeting and always subject to unforeseen forces.

Yet these two principles in life—power and pleasure— have been the focus of much attention and analysis in psychotherapy, and have been used as a platform for designing and managing both organizations and work. As we have already discussed, the father of psychoanalysis, Sigmund Freud, weighed in on the pleasure principle; Alfred Adler, also known as the founder of individual psychology, weighed in on the will to power. A huge body of work has gone into defining us by these principles—all of which require outside forces to come into play.

It is here, in the vast exploration of our inner and outer lives, that Frankl's will to meaning rises above and distinguishes itself from the will to pleasure and the will to power. The will to meaning comes from *within*. Only we ourselves can find it, control it, and fulfill it. It is meaning that sustains us throughout our lives, no matter how little or how much power and pleasure come our way. Most important of all, meaning sustains us through any pain and suffering that we must endure.

In his book, *Full Catastrophe Living,* Jon Kabat-Zinn writes about staying connected to our original wholeness no matter what the challenges to our health, well-being, and welfare. His book explores the lives of many people for whom life-threatening illness became a transforming experience. They connected, not only to others in a way that anchored them in love, acceptance, and forgiveness, but also to themselves. Some survived and triumphed over illness, others didn't. They all deepened their experience in ways that honored meaning in their lives as well as in death.

When we take the time to cultivate our relationship to our original self, all our experience becomes grounded in meaning. This was true for Frankl when he observed the behavior of those imprisoned in the Nazi concentration camps; it was true for those interviewed throughout Kabat-Zinn's book; and it's true for anyone who has survived tragedy and allowed their grief to break open their heart to tenderness. When tenderness prevails, we love and forgive ourselves and others. When the opposite happens, when bitterness seals our hearts shut, we are isolated from ourselves, from others, and, ultimately, from meaning itself.

If we take the time to think about our friends, we all know someone who has survived tragic loss or similar fate yet somehow retained deep cheerfulness and optimism as the way through life. One person I know, Charlotte, recently lost a 21-year-old son who had suffered from autism. I had spoken with Charlotte only months before her son's death about the challenges and, yes, burden of raising an autistic child. Charlotte described the experience candidly, noting that it was not always easy for either her or her husband over so many years. She even recalled reading Frankl's book, *Man's Search for Meaning*, on several occasions during this time and underscored its influence on her thinking and actions during some of the most difficult moments. Indeed, Charlotte was able to find deeper meaning in her experience as a parent, no matter how difficult the challenge, and she learned much about her own humanness through her relationship with her disabled son. And when her son died suddenly at such an early age, it became clear that his life and legacy was the ground out of which the rest of Charlotte's life would be shaped. Significantly, it has become a life shaped by love, generosity, meaningful work, and social activism.

But in our culture there's a long tradition of separating work from play, profession from recreation. We draw arbitrary boundaries around our work lives, sometimes thinking that it protects our loved ones from stress, sometimes to protect ourselves from the stress. Yet our work, whether we run a company, drive a cab, make a quilt, cook a meal, or clean a hotel room, is a reflection of meaning in our lives.

When we clean a hotel room, cleanliness is next to holiness; we are participating in an ancient ritual that honors the sacred nature of a human being. In tribal, nomadic cultures, cleanliness and beautiful surroundings are part of daily life. The dirt floor is swept; the art is carved on the mud walls. Often when the conditions are most challenging and sparse, the people are colorful in dress and jewelry. They themselves bring beauty to their austere surroundings.

In Tibet, in Navajo country, in India, the brilliant dress and vibrant jewelry worn by "impoverished" people celebrates the deep meaning in their lives as well as their awareness of their "riches." It's interesting that in the 1980s in the United States, when commercial wealth was on the rise, the grunge movement became the expression of our youth. Perhaps there is a kind of freedom in having little in the way of material possessions that liberates us to celebrate ourselves more deeply. Perhaps material excess, which in many ways is closely associated both to the will to pleasure and the will to power, hinders our ability to celebrate our spiritual awareness and the inherent beauty and meaning in our lives.

In Buddhist tradition, the cook and the temple cleaner may be the most important teachers in the community. They are honed by their humbleness, by their attention to the daily details of life. Their attention creates meaning and it is this, not their talks and teachings, that draws students to them. Sometimes the cook and the cleaner appear as Buddhist jesters; they play with their humble roles, hide behind them, watching for the ripe students to come their way. They are cleaners and cooks in waiting. If you talk to those in the service professions about their work, their stories will often amaze you. They see things that the rest of us don't. They experience human nature, often from behind a mask of professional detachment, in ways that most of us rarely get the chance to do.

These days we are used to thinking about financial independence as the pathway to freedom. Indeed, I remember a recent advertising campaign in Canada that was called "Freedom 55," that promised not only financial independence beginning at age 55 but also the lure of *freedom* to do whatever you would want for the rest of your life. With the average life-span increasing for both men and women, I wondered what this kind of "freedom" would ultimately mean for such young retirees. What would they do with—and for—the rest of their lives?

Interestingly, there is evidence that older Canadians are spurning retirement, choosing the office and meaningful work over 24/7 bridge and golf. And not necessarily because they have to. Such older workers, in fact, may be offering aging baby boomers a peek into their own futures. In a 1998 survey of boomers sponsored by the American Association of Retired People (AARP), some 80 percent said that they would keep on working beyond traditional retirement age. Although the reasons for working beyond traditional retirement age are many, here is what one older worker has to say: "It's important to stay busy, to have goals and plans. There are still plenty of depressed retired people who have nothing to do. It's like they're waiting to die, and it's such a waste."[4]

Once again, we are reminded of the many twists and turns that occur naturally, although not always seamlessly, as we explore the labyrinth of meaning in our work lives. The metaphor for freedom is also true in another important respect. Living and working from the *inside out* is a choice, both of attitude and action. As we learned in the previous chapter, true freedom is not "just another word for nothing left to lose," as the late singer Janis Joplin, once suggested in song lyrics written by Kris Kristofferson. Whether we like it or not, we are not only free to choose but also responsible for our choices. So, if we decide to put our real aspirations—be they personal or work-related—in a lock box with the expectation that we'll some day return to fetch them, that's our choice. And, just as important, we must be prepared to live with the fact that we may never return to the contents of our lock box, nor realize our will to meaning!

As prisoners of our thoughts, we can't always see very clearly through the bars of our metaphorical prison cell. And to see more clearly, we first must be willing to "go inward":

> It's time to go inward, take a look at myself.
> Time to make the most of the time that I've got left.
> Prison bars imagined are no less solid steel.
> Rodney Crowell[5]

Sadly, we frequently miss opportunities to enjoy the "spaciousness" that already exists within us to feel authentic meaning in our lives and work. Frankl would say that only if we remain aware of and committed to *meaningful* values will we be able to fully enjoy this spaciousness. Yet how can we ensure that we will remain aware of such important values in our lives? Let me now introduce you to a simple exercise that you can use for a meaningful purpose.

The exercise is based on Frankl's invitation, in his book *The Doctor and the Soul,* to spread our lives out before us like a beautiful mountain range. My version of this Mountain Range Exercise goes like this: First, ask yourself (and feel free to invite your co-workers to participate) to look out over your work life as one would look out over a mountain range. Whom would you place on the peaks before you? In other words, who are the people who have influenced your career and work life? These people may include authors, teachers, employers, leaders, or people in your personal life who have mentored (or even loved) you, or whom you have loved or otherwise admired. You can use paper, colored pens, or markers to sketch out your mountain range and write on the peaks the names of the people who have influenced you.

Now, encourage yourself to look for *recurring values*, that is, values that surface more than once. You may, for instance, recall the empowerment of a particular teacher or supervisor. Explore the key values of the various people who had contributed significantly to your work life. Focus on those values that you may have incorporated into your own value system. Which of these values are the most *positive*, the most *meaningful*? To which of these values have you been most committed over the course of your career or work life? To which of these values are you *now* most committed?

As you can see, this Mountain Range Exercise helps you look at your work life from a different, and unique, perspective. Through it you can discover recurring values, recognize your own uniqueness, and broaden your view about your work and personal lives. It is also an unfolding exercise, a new way of looking at life, that can help you discover the essence of your will to meaning at work.

In America, we live surrounded by more material wealth than any other society in the world. Yet we are restless, unhappy, disconnected, both from others and from our inner lives. Our suicide rates for young people are increasing and there is a growing divide between those with wealth and those on the economic margins. We have all the resources necessary for widespread health-care and economic stability, yet the spiraling discrepancies between rich and poor, the value placed on money for its own sake, is taking the place of our respect for one another in particular, and for humanity in general.

*The truth is that as the struggle for survival has subsided, the question
has emerged: survival for what? Even more people today have the
means to live but no meaning to live for.*[6]

These are dire times. Yet they are born of plenty. In his
work, Frankl observed that as the struggle for basic physical
survival of our human species subsided, the question has
emerged: Survival for what? Even as more people today have
the financial means to live they are struggling with the question: What are we living *for?* In the face of material abun-
dance, our inner emptiness, or "existential vacuum" in
Frankl's words, has become ever more pressing.

These observations were reinforced in an article that
appeared in the *Utne Reader On-Line*, the Web-based medi-
um of one of the best-known alternative publications in the
United States. According to the authors, life in the postmodern world, especially in what they call "America the
Blue," displays certain characteristics and influences that
appear very much like manifestations of Frankl's existential
vacuum:

*Why am I sad? Why am I anxious? Why can't I love? The answer, per-
haps, lies deep in our collective subconscious. The route to the surface
passes through the postmodern hall of mirrors. The trip looks forbidding.
And yet it is a worthwhile excursion. Think of it as trying to solve the
tantalizing psychothriller of your own life, the ultimate existential who-
dunit . . . Like it or not, we humans are stuck in a permanent crisis of
meaning, a dark room from which we can never escape. Postmodernism
pulls the philosophical carpet out from under us and leaves us in an existential void.*[7]

Viktor Frankl, one of the world's most profound and *true*
optimists, would disagree vehemently with the notion that

"we can never escape" the dark room of meaninglessness. Perhaps postmodernism has fallen prey to its own beliefs, or lack thereof, in its nihilistic analysis, which basically devalues the meaning of all life. Postmodernism relies on modernism to lay claim to its own existence. For most of the world, modernism is still a dream, if indeed, that is, modernism can be defined by such "modern" ideas as sufficient food and shelter. When we let ourselves be defined by the analytical arrogance of postmodern thinkers, injustice is served all-round.

Frankl developed and practiced Logotherapy as a way to find and open the windows and doors of rooms of despair for everyone—from the death-row inmate and the concentration-camp survivor to the CEO, the cab or bus driver, and the postmodern philosophy professor. He designed a framework of *being* and *doing* that offers an entirely new design for our lives—rooms to live and work in that have both innate meaning *and* a view. He provided a disciplined approach for discovering meaning in even the most catastrophic of circumstances—an approach rooted firmly in his profound personal experience.

In addition to the feelings of *inner emptiness* that seem to exist among greater numbers of our working (and, for that matter, retired) population, more people feel trapped at work—and perhaps in life generally. How do employers and employees, as well as the citizens of the so-called "free agent nation,"[8] deal with these complex issues? Unfortunately, many companies only provide employees with the "illusion" of feeling free and alive, as opposed to feeling trapped, at work. Even periodic pay increases and other financial rewards may only have this kind of illusory effect, especially if employers, albeit unconsciously, use such instruments in a way that fosters worker attention solely on the paycheck rather than on the reason(s) for their work. In this regard, it is perhaps worthwhile to point out here that Frankl viewed the "will to money" as a primitive form of the will to power.

In basing his company's development on meaningful goals, Tom's of Maine founder Tom Chappell also brought deep personal meaning to his life. He created a company that invites all of its employees to share in a meaning-based bottom line. The company not only observes ethical environmental practices in the development of its products, it also gives 10 percent of pretax profits to addressing community concerns in Maine, its corporate base, and around the world. And volunteerism is allocated at 5 percent of the employees' paid time. This commitment reflects more than traditional corporate social responsibility concerns; it encompasses ethical and soulful values that honor the emotional, intellectual, and spiritual life of both internal and external stakeholders, as well as the health and well-being of both the planet and the bottom line. In short, it is a partnership of meaning.

But what if we are working in a company or corporation that isn't as enlightened as Tom's of Maine? How do we acknowledge the ultimate worthiness of life in our work? If we step back from the superficial perspective of "a job equals a paycheck," we can begin to search for meaning: How many opportunities do we have each day to connect meaningfully with others? Do we take those moments and make real contact? Do we honor the people we meet? Do we take the time to appreciate the power we have to bring meaning to our relationships? Do we honor our own time? Do we look for new, creative ways to perceive and approach our work? Are we experiencing our connections on many levels at once or are we limiting our experience to getting to the end of the day and the next paycheck? Metaphorically speaking, do we run from the parking lot to work each day or do we bless the moment that TGIF[9] arrives?

In his lectures and speeches, and in a book published initially in 1977, Frankl passionately warned us about an "unheard cry for meaning." He characterized this as coming from a combination of three things: depression, aggression, and addiction. It is a cry that can only be fully understood in light of the underlying existential void. It is a collective cry that perhaps is more prevalent today than when first identified by Frankl. And it is a cry that is not going away.

Stress, for instance, is killing us. "Rage" has become a commonly defined social phenomenon, whether it's road rage, rage at work, at school, or at home, or even in the parking lot. "Going postal" is a phrase all too common and all too peculiar to these times. We are becoming more and more cynical and skeptical about everything from corporate and governmental motives to the trustworthiness of our friends and neighbors. Our educational systems are failing us and our young people are becoming alienated and depressed. It's a collective "unheard cry for meaning" that belies the mask of our have-a-nice-day culture. It's only by hearing this cry, in our own voices and in those of others, that having a meaningful day will become the measurement of our daily life.

In his book *The Re-Enchantment of Everyday Life*, former Catholic monk and professor of religion and psychology
Thomas Moore explores the possibility of experiencing
enchantment at work. He writes about the Roman god, Mer-
cury, "the divine patron of commerce." In ancient Rome,
business was considered sacred. Work, money, the arts, religion, and philosophy were integrated into daily life. Moore
writes:

> *Economics is the law of life, and in fact this word also has deep mean-*
> *ing, coming from* oikos, *Greek for home or temple . . . and* nomos,
> *meaning management, custom and law. . . . Business involves all*
> *aspects of managing our home, whether the family house or the planet,*
> *and therefore has to do with survival, fulfillment, community, and*
> *meaning.*[10]

Finding enchantment at work might sound to some
people like an exercise in futility, but it can and does happen. And, when it does, the ripple effect through the world
of work can be monumental. To be enchanted means to be
soulfully involved, to be beside ourselves with excitement,
gratitude, appreciation—to be full of possibility. When we
bring this meaning-focused sensibility to our work, creativity
flourishes and so does productivity.

For example, take the case of Skaltek, a major equipment manufacturer based in Stockholm, Sweden. Listen to
the words of Öystein Skalleberg, the founder of Skaltek, as
he describes his philosophy about people and work:

> *Every human being is a Leonardo da Vinci. The only problem is that he*
> *doesn't know it. His parents didn't know it, and they didn't treat him*

like a Leonardo. Therefore he didn't become like a Leonardo. That's my basic theory.[11]

Significantly, Skalleberg practices what he preaches. At Skaltek, the company doesn't employ job titles so as to avoid the practice of conferring some privileged status to certain people, and each employee's business card only carries pertinent contact information along with a photo. Once, when Skalleberg was asked about this policy on job titles, he responded that, if he *were* to give his employees a job title, it would be something like "Leonardo da Vinci" or "Unlimited Possibilities" rather than the job titles that are employed by most companies.

In addition, there are no cookie-cutter job descriptions, and all workers who help build a machine at Skaltek actually add their individual signature to the final product. In this way, there is not only a direct line from the customer to everyone involved in product development but also an emphasis on total quality management that is completely transparent. There are even more radical attributes of the working environment at Skaltek, such as an annual employee appraisal process that involves the use of randomly selected performance review teams. According to Skalleberg, since no one knows who will be conducting their performance review each year, "Everybody smiles in all directions!" Skalleberg also has a revolutionary formula for building a company culture in the postmodern era: "Confidence is the start of it, Joy is a part of it, Love is the heart of it." Now, doesn't Skaltek sound like a company with a meaning-focused philosophy about bringing enchantment to work?

The salvation of man is through love and in love. I understood how a
man who has nothing left in this world still may know bliss, be it only
for a brief moment, in the contemplation of his beloved.[12]

"An enchanted life is good for business, even if it requires a turnabout in values and vision," writes Moore.[13] His "proof" comes from evidence of the opposite perspective: how the lack of enchantment in our work leads to emotional and physical distress, lowered morale, decreased productivity, and dispirited employees. In short, if we can't bring our soulfulness to work, eventually we suffer. And so does business.

When there's soulfulness at the top of a company, the trickle-down effect can be explosive. In 1995, when fire destroyed the Malden Mills factory in Massachusetts, 3,000 people were instantly out of jobs. But not for long. As he watched his factory burn, Aaron Feuerstein, president and CEO of the company, decided then and there that it was not the end of Malden Mills. The first thing he did was keep all 3,000 workers on the payroll with full benefits for three months. There was nowhere for them to work, but in his heart, mind, and soul he knew that it was unconscionable to put 3,000 people out on the streets. The company was directly or indirectly involved on every level in the community. It would be a death blow not only to the employees and their families but also to everyone in the cities of Lawrence and Methuen, Massachusetts. And because Malden Mills supplied high-tech fabrics for products sold by outdoor apparel retailers, such as L.L. Bean and Lands' End, his customers were at risk, too.

It cost millions of dollars to keep all 3,000 workers on

the payroll and put the company into bankruptcy, but Feuerstein prevailed. He risked everything—his money, his reputation, his business. He believed in his employees and they, in return, believed in him. He set up temporary plants in old warehouses and the collective response was astounding.

"Before the fire that plant produced 130,000 yards a week", said Feuerstein. "A few weeks after the fire, it was up to 230,000 yards. Our people became very creative. They were willing to work 25 hours a day."

Feuerstein instinctively valued his work force; he invested in their well-being immediately and with great risk. Then he put his will to the task of meaningfully rebuilding his company. It was the phoenix of possibility rising out of the ashes. The employees, blue-collar and white-collar alike, rose to the occasion and committed themselves to the collective good. In 2003, the company came out of bankruptcy.

When meaning is honored at the top of any organization, it can be easy to bring meaning to our jobs. It's a natural reflection of meaningful values. If we are valued and appreciated, if our well-being is nurtured, we feel a part of a meaningful whole. But soulfulness can trickle up, too. It might be more difficult to honor meaning at work when there's little manifesting from above, but it also might be more important to do so.

We are in a crisis of corporate accountability. In many companies, there is no trickle-down soulfulness because the forces operating the companies are so distant and diffused that there can be no meaningful link down through the ranks. The financial bottom line becomes the only thing that defines meaning and, when this happens, the ethical and moral decisions that are at the heart of capitalism are obliterated. They have to come from *all* of us as individuals, no matter what our role in the company.

When we choose meaning in the workplace, we pay attention to everything around us. We choose respect, kindness, and courtesy. We choose justice and fair play. We bring our own ethical and moral decision making to our jobs and we find ways to have an impact. Sometimes it might be by simple recognition of our co-workers; sometimes by writing a letter expressing our observations and concerns; sometimes through organizing support for a constructive change. Most of all, by understanding that when we ourselves bring meaning to work, we bring with us the possibility of meaningful change in the workplace.

A financial bottom line is not motivated by ethical and moral decisions; *people* are motivated by ethical and moral decisions. When people are replaced by money as the presiding force behind decision making, that is, the will to money or power, we have no choice but to become aware of the implications and do something about it. The most we can do is bring meaning out into the light. By refusing to be held a *prisoner of our thoughts*, we can bring our will to meaning to work, and it will *mean* something.

(Meaning Moment) Recall a situation in your work life in which you were challenged to examine your commitment to meaningful values or goals (this may even be your situation today). Perhaps you were faced with a job assignment that wasn't in alignment with your personal values. Perhaps you were just unhappy with the work that you were doing. How did you first come to recognize this challenge? What, if anything, did you actually *do* about it? As you think about the situation now, what did you *learn* from it? In particular, what did you learn about your commitment to meaningful values and goals, that is, your will to meaning? In hindsight, what would you have done differently in this situation?

 Meaning Question: How do *you* ensure that you remain committed to meaningful values and goals, and thereby realize your *will to meaning*, at work or in the workplace?

FOR FURTHER REFLECTION

Think about the underlying values and goals that characterize your work or workplace. In what way(s) do they reflect Freud's "will to pleasure," Adler's "will to power," and Frankl's "will to meaning"?

Detect the Meaning of Life's Moments

*Live as if you were living already for the second time and as if you had
acted the first time as wrongly as you are about to act now!*[1]

Michelle had recently celebrated her fiftieth birthday but
was not quite ready to admit that she had reached the half-
century mark and was dreading retirement age. In fact, she
was not a happy camper and not inclined to celebrate anything in her life. Twice divorced and the single mother of
two Generation X'ers, Michelle's personal life, as far as she
was concerned, left much to be desired, and she didn't feel
much better about her work life either. Since her last mar-
riage ended, she had been having a very difficult time hold-
ing any kind of steady employment. Whenever she did find a
job that seemed worthwhile, it always soured quickly. Over
and over, Michelle would find herself "stressed out" at work;
always, of course, for some reason that had nothing to do
with herself—a poor boss, lazy co-workers, unclear job
description, lack of support, and so on. Consequently, she

was never satisfied with her present work situation and certainly never imagined that she could have a meaningful career path.

Because she was also stressed out at home, Michelle was experiencing a double whammy with no end in sight. She seemed consumed by a need to put out fires at work and at home, with nothing in reserve for determining the root causes of her anguish. As she became increasingly depressed over her life situation, Michelle's tendency to externalize the reasons for her plight hardened into a suit of impenetrable armor. Over time, Michelle became oblivious to her own role and responsibility—as co-creator of her miserable "reality"—and effectively lost touch with the meaning of life's precious moments because she was too busy complaining about what life had been doing *to* her. In her mind, life had dealt her a bad hand, so at this stage of her existence there was nothing to do but bear the suffering and complain loud enough so that everyone around her—her family, friends, co-workers, and the like—would hear her cries of pain.

"The meaning of it all is that there is no meaning," said the golfer Walter Hogan in the movie *The Legend of Bagger Vance*. Michelle would agree, for the search for meaning had no value to her. Her life was meaningless and most likely would continue to be meaningless—unless perhaps some sort of miracle came her way—for she wasn't inclined to search for anything different. Perhaps Michelle was simply experiencing a mid-life crisis, you ask? Perhaps. Whatever the reason, ironically Michelle had chosen to take an early retirement from life by giving up on her search for meaning.

We don't create meaning; we find it. And we can't find

it if we don't look for it. Meaning comes to us in all shapes and sizes. Sometimes it looms big in our lives; sometimes it slips in almost unobserved. Sometimes we miss a meaningful moment entirely until days, months, or even years go by and then suddenly something that once seemed insignificant becomes a pivotal, life-changing moment. Sometimes, too, it is the collective meaning of many moments that finally catches our mind's eye; as if we weave together a living quilt from patches of moments that, by themselves, would have passed us by unnoticed. And, although we are not always aware of it, meaning, Frankl would say, is in every present moment. It goes without saying—wherever we go. All we have to do, in daily life and at work, is to wake up to meaning and take notice.

> The true meaning of life is to be discovered in the world rather than within man or his own psyche, as if it were a closed system.[2]

It sounds easy but these days it can feel almost impossible to do. Our sound-bite society speeds up reality to such an extent that stopping to smell the roses seems archaic, like some sentimental activity from an earlier era. In an era of "fast companies," it is like we have forgotten how to slow down and how to reflect. We're more likely to stop and use our cell phone, or check our email. Time is getting away from us, and so is meaning. And, like time, we notice meaning when there isn't much left. We wake up one day, or don't sleep one night, and suddenly our exhaustion, the fragmentation of our lives, the unrelenting pace of things, leaves us bereft of meaning. What is it all about, we wonder?

There is no answer to the big question unless we

discover answers to the smaller ones: What are we doing? Why are we doing it? What do our lives mean to us? What does our work mean? Every day our lives are rich with meaningful answers. But only when we stop long enough to appreciate it will meaning bloom in our lives. We have to really be there to detect and know meaning, and most of the time we are on our way somewhere else. The frenzy of activity in our lives—at work and at home—is challenging the very nature of our existence. And if we don't stop long enough to sniff out our own existence, we turn meaning into an impossible dream.

So before we go on the hunt for meaning at work, we have to know that meaning means something. Our lives are full of it. The rhythm of existence—the tides, the stars, the seasons, the ebb and flow of life, the miraculous being-ness of it all—is always available to us at every given moment. There are no exceptions. Every astronaut who ever returned from outer space attests to the great miracle that is life on this earth. All of science conspires to get men and women into space, but it is when they return to earth that the miracle really begins. They see the planet suspended in the vastness of space, its continents and clouds luminous in an unfathomable universe, all life hanging by some invisible thread of possibility. Their jobs take them to cosmic heights of achievement, yet it is being back on earth that brings them to their knees.

The thirteenth-century Sufi poet Rumi writes, "It's never too late to bend and kiss the earth." The meaningfulness of life, as we know it and don't know it, is manifest everywhere on this fragile planet. Wherever we are and whatever we do, it is this very existence of life that calls us to meaning. How are we inviting life into our lives? How are we bending and kissing this earthly experience? How are we acknowledging meaning in our lives, through our work, at our jobs? The answers are as varied as our needs.

The distinction between what has professional credibility and what doesn't is insidious. Our lives are pregnant with meaning and therefore everything we do, in every moment, has meaning. We have the freedom to make decisions out of love for whatever is in our hearts. When we stop to look at the reasons for our decisions, we will always find meaning. But it takes time to reflect; and even though there's as much time as there ever was, it seems as if less and less is available to us. Taking time back is the first step in opening ourselves to meaning. But where has all the time gone?

To begin with, technology is a great time stealer. I confess to remembering the time before telephone answering machines. People either got hold of one another, or they didn't. There were no cell phones attaching themselves to our every move, nor was there email or voice mail. People at home and at work took messages and left notes—on paper, no less! As a result there was spaciousness to decide when, and even whether, we returned the call. There was spaciousness to think, to consider, and to contemplate our decisions—both simple and complex.

In twenty-five years, the entire world of communication has turned things around. If we don't respond instantly to an email or a cell-phone call it can be tantamount to personal betrayal or professional ineptitude. Technology, which is supposed to make life easier, has added a whole new layer of obligations. If we're not really careful, it controls us.

There are, of course, good things about it all: a revival of the written word via email; access to enormous amounts of information via the Web; greater accessibility via cell phones in case of emergencies; and, thanks to voice mail, no more missed messages of importance. But unless we do so purposefully, there is nowhere to hide from it all.

I know many people, including family members, friends, and colleagues, who are completely addicted to their cell phone. They take it everywhere: on walks, shopping, driving (even where it is against the law), to restaurants, and, yes, to the movies, where, regrettably, they often forget to turn it off. Their cell phone seems not only to function as an appendage of their body, it provides them with a symbol of their place in the world. In short, "Can you hear me now?" has become one of their mantras for living and they don't go anywhere without their cell phone. While *they* may remain "connected" at all times, one of the unintended consequences of this technology is that so are we. Think about how many times you have been forced to listen to a cell phone conversation in public—details about business or personal matters that you really didn't need or want to hear?

What about our reliance on email as a way of staying connected and, more insidiously, *obligated*? How many people do you know who appear to be *hard-wired* to their email account? They couldn't imagine a day going by without checking it? I suspect this is true of more and more of us; we are linked to outside obligations in ways that define much of the time of our lives. There is great possibility in this and also great burden. It's extremely important that we recognize the difference and know when we are responding in ways that undermine our connection to meaning.

It all comes down to awareness. In this regard, it has been said that "it is more important to be aware than it is to be smart."[3] To be aware is to know meaning. To be aware takes time. If our lives are propelled by nothing but things piling up to respond to or the passive preoccupation with television, we lose out on meaning. We have to see, hear, smell, touch, and taste meaning if it's going to exist in our lives.

> All that is good and beautiful in the past is safely preserved in that past. On the other hand, so long as life remains, all guilt and all evil is still "redeemable". . . . this is not the case of a finished film . . . or an already existent film which is merely being unrolled. Rather, the film of this world is just being "shot." Which means nothing more or less than that the future—happily—still remains to be shaped; that is, it is at the disposal of man's responsibility.[4]

There are as many shades of meaning as there are colors. And nobody can determine meaning for someone else. Detecting the meaning of life's moments is a personal responsibility, one that cannot be simply delegated to another. This is the case no matter how much we would like to do so. Like it or not, if we are aware that we're in a lousy job but we need to pay the rent, the job has meaning. This doesn't mean that we resign ourselves to lifelong lousy jobs; it means there is meaning in the one we have right now. If we hate our boss because she's demanding and unappreciative, we can either be demanding and unappreciative right back or try to discover a life lesson in our predicament. Maybe the boss is trying too hard to succeed; maybe we're hearing a parental voice from our past and not her at all; maybe we have an opportunity to practice our diplomatic skills with a difficult person. Or, maybe we really are in a job that is not right for us!

In *Man's Search for Meaning*, Frankl describes a case in which he met with a high-ranking American diplomat at his office in Vienna, presumably to continue psychoanalytic treatment that this person had begun five years earlier in New York City.[5] At the outset, Dr. Frankl asked the diplomat why he thought that he should undergo analysis, and why it had started in the first place. It turned out that this "patient" had been discontented with his career and found it most difficult to comply with American foreign policy. His analyst, however, had told him again and again that he should to try to reconcile himself with his father, because his employer (the U.S. government) and his superiors were "nothing but" father figures and, consequently, his dissatisfaction with his job was due to hatred he unconsciously harbored toward his father.

For five years, the diplomat had been prompted to accept this interpretation of his plight and he became increasingly confused—unable to see the forest of reality for the trees of symbols and images. After a few interviews with Dr. Frankl, it was clear that the diplomat's real problem was that his *will to meaning* was being frustrated by his vocation and that he actually longed to be engaged in some other kind of work. In the end, he decided to give up his profession and embark on another one, which, as it turned out, proved to be very gratifying to him. In truth, his anguish had not been because of his father but a result of his *own* inability to choose work that had true meaning for him.

If we open ourselves to being aware of the many possibilities, we open ourselves to meaning. We also have to open ourselves to our own integrity and authenticity, which is akin to living and working with meaning. Unfortunately, there's not always support for us to do so, especially in the workplace. To be sure, the roots of this complex issue run deep into the soil (and soul) of our postmodern culture. Our integrity, our search for deeper purpose and meaning can take a bruising when held up against the search for more and more money. Think, for instance, about the injury we all feel when the media exposes corporate scandals and the collateral damage that always accompanies them. To be sure, it's important to know what we are up against when we take the time and the awareness to contemplate the meaning of meaning in our lives.

It is life itself that invites us to discover meaning, and when we live our lives with awareness, we express meaning in everything we do. *Webster's Third New International Dictionary* lists more than twenty definitions for the word *work* and more than a hundred other words or phrases that begin with the word *work*. But it's the first definition with its two small root words, *to do*, that illustrates the meaning of them all. Whatever we *do* has meaning, whether it's a workout or a work of art.

> *Life retains its meaning under any conditions. It remains meaningful literally up to its last moment, up to one's last breath.*[6]

Knowing why we do things, however, is essential. Knowing why we do things is the beginning of real freedom and real meaning in our lives. If we delve deep enough we'll get to the two things that motivate us most: love and conscience. Frankl described these as intuitive capabilities: things we do without thinking, things that define us at our deepest level. "The truth," he wrote in *Man's Search for Meaning*, "is that love is the ultimate and the highest goal to which man can aspire."

It's not always easy to trace where love and conscience come into play in our lives, but if we stop a moment to explore our decisions, they surface clearly: We work nights so we can be with our kids in the morning and see them off to school. We grow vegetables organically to provide healthy food for the community. We operate a small business that offers employment to three people year-round in a difficult economy. We write poems and send them to friends. We consult with others to help them more effectively cope with stress. We teach sailing to inner-city kids. We manage a corporation with an emphasis on fair wages for workers abroad. We make quilts for families who are homeless. We work at a job we don't love because it gives us time to do something we do love. We organize affordable housing in our community. We donate a thousand dollars to a local charity. We put a dollar in an outstretched hand. We build energy-efficient straw bale houses. We wait tables so we can be onstage, raise our kids, feed our dog, pay the light bill. It all comes down to love and conscience. And when we see how our world is connected in this way, we can name "why" and know meaning.

Do you remember from the last chapter Öystein Skalleberg's revolutionary formula for building a company culture? To refresh your memory, here it is again: "Confidence is the start of it, Joy is a part of it, *Love* is the heart of it." How many organizations, in any sector, do you know that place the notion of love (not romantic love) at the heart of its credo? Now you know why the Skaltek work environment is unique and why Skalleberg's formula is so revolutionary.

The world is full of good deeds and the opportunity to do good deeds. When we don't do them, it's often out of fear. Fear of losing something: our status, our loved one, our job, our security, our sense of identity; our place in the world. The notion of fear at work and in the workplace has received considerable attention over the years. In fact, "driving fear out of the workplace" has long been a core principle of total quality management, but it remains a formidable challenge that has yet to be resolved.[7] Against this backdrop, approaches to assist individuals work *through* fear, as well as to help executives and managers become *fearless*, are readily available to meet this challenge.[8]

In the 1991 film *Defending Your Life*, director/writer Albert Brooks plays Dan Miller, a successful business executive who takes delivery on a new BMW and plows it into a bus while trying to adjust the CD player. Dan finds himself dead, but awake, in a place called Judgment City, a heavenly way station that Roger Ebert, the film critic, described as "run along the lines that would be recommended by a good MBA program." And it is in Judgment City's courtroom where Dan must try to explain and *defend* his life, particularly those moments, shown on video, when fear was most evident in his actions. Now consider the following dialogue that takes place between Dan and his defense attorney, Bob Diamond (played by Rip Torn):

Bob Diamond: Being from earth as you are and using as little of your brain as you do, your life has pretty much been devoted to dealing with fear.

Dan Miller: It has?

Bob Diamond: Everybody on earth deals with fear. That's what little brains do.

. . .

Bob Diamond: Did you ever have friends whose stomachs hurt?

Dan Miller: Every one of them.

Bob Diamond: It's fear. Fear is like a giant fog. It sits on your brain and blocks everything. Real feeling, true happiness, real joy, they can't get through that fog. But you lift it and buddy you're in for the ride of your life.

What lessons about detecting the meaning of life's moments are illustrated in this dialogue? For one thing, fear is depicted as the metaphorical "fog" that blinds one's search for meaning. Fear, in this context, relates to our inability to actualize creative expression, to experience new situations and relationships with others, and to change our attitude toward something or someone. According to Frankl, these are all sources of authentic meaning. I should point out that courage is not the absence of fear but the willingness and ability to walk through the fear—to tread, if you will, into the darkness of life's labyrinth of meaning. And it is during the worst of times, including inescapable hardship and suffering, that our courage is put to its greatest test.

Over and over again, from those who have lost everything we learn that the worst of times is often the catalyst for the best of times. What we learn from Viktor Frankl's life and work is that even the most profound grief and intolerable circumstances can open us to meaning. And so can even the smallest of moments. All we have to do is take back the time in our lives, pay attention to the details and know "why."

> In the concentration camps, . . . in this living laboratory and on this testing ground, we watched and witnessed some of our comrades behave like swine while others behaved like saints. Man has both potentials within himself; which one is actualized depends on decisions but not on conditions.[9]

Sometimes we have to approach the search for meaning from another perspective. We have to know we don't know and start from there. We have to let meaning find us. This seems to be difficult as we grow older, especially at midlife when we encounter a critical crossroads on the path to meaning. Rather than having a so-called midlife crisis, writes Mark Gerzon in his book *Coming Into Our Own: Understanding the Adult Metamorphosis*, we can begin a search for deeper love, purpose, and meaning that becomes possible in life's second half.[10] Envisioning life, including our work life, as a quest, not a crisis, after midlife is an opportunity that holds great potency for all, including the growing number of baby boomers on the horizon of old age.

With increases in life expectancy and leisure time in their postretirement years, more people are beginning to ask the existential question: "Is that all there is?" At the same time, there are more people who are "retiring" at an earlier age for various reasons. Some people retire voluntarily, while others have been forced into retirement through downsizing, mergers, and the like. The increased amount of time that is becoming available to people under each of these scenarios is raising awareness of many meaning-centered questions. Indeed, the stories of "retired" thirty-somethings from Silicon Valley (while they obviously are now rare occurrences due to shifts in economic conditions) illustrate the dichotomy that can exist between success and fulfillment. Isolation, depression, and other symptoms of these lost souls among the *nouveau riche* appear to run counter to conventional wisdom. How could monetary wealth, and the time to do whatever you would want, be associated with a lack of personal meaning?

Retirement at later stages of life demands similar attention to questions of meaning, especially due to the extended life expectancy that workers in Western society now enjoy. Why is it, for instance, that some workers seem to "retire" from life while others simply transform or redesign themselves for new and meaningful challenges in living and work? The life and legacy of Viktor Frankl have taught us, in no uncertain terms, to approach the aging process from a position of personal strength and in a way that respects the dignity of the human spirit. The post-midlife years of Frankl, who had not retired at over 90 years of age, provides a window for us to see how important the will to meaning can actually be throughout one's lifetime.

All things being equal, I suspect that the new "balanced scorecard" of the twenty-first century will be concerned more with success at making a *life* than it will be about making a living. Hence, as people become more aware of their own mortality, as well as their commitment to *meaningful* values (i.e., their will to meaning), they will be more likely to consider the kind of personal legacy they would like to leave behind. To Frankl, this kind of questioning is a manifestation of being truly human: "No ant, no bee, no animal will ever raise the question of whether or not its existence has a meaning, but man does. It's his privilege that he cares for a meaning to his existence. He is not only searching for such a meaning, but he is even entitled to it . . . After all, it's a sign of intellectual honesty and sincerity."[11]

By reflecting upon our existence and seeking to detect the meaning of life's moments, we also create the opportunity to draft our personal legacy, albeit as a work in progress. There are a number of simple and practical exercises that can be used for this purpose; let me now introduce you to some of them. Because I am blessed with living in the mountains of northern New Mexico, I like to call the first exercise High Altitude Thinking.

Imagine that you are sitting high on a mountain peak overlooking *your life*. From this distance, you can see all of the roads that you have taken, all of the stops that you have made, all of the people that you have encountered, all of the things that you have done or experienced in your life. Like a mapmaker, draw the map of your life, using various symbols to highlight the milestones in each of the above areas. Ask yourself the significance or meaning of each milestone; after all, you've identified it as such, so now you should be able to determine why it is what it is. Next, weave together the pieces of your life's map, referring to the milestones as the fabric to be used, and create a quilt that symbolizes your life and work. Embedded in your life/work quilt are the threads of your personal legacy.

Another exercise that can be used as a catalyst for you to reflect upon your life, including your work life, and help you chart your path to a meaningful existence takes a much different approach. Like Albert Brook's character Dan Miller in the movie *Defending Your Life*, imagine that you have died. However, rather than imagining yourself in Judgment City, put yourself in the position of having to write your own obituary for the local newspaper. What would you say? In other words, how do you want to be remembered? What are the most important things that you experienced in your life? Since the newspaper editor has given you a one-page space limitation, you must be as clear and succinct about your message as possible.

An alternative to the Obituary Exercise is depicted in the Eulogy Exercise, on the next page. In this exercise, you are asked to fill in the blanks on the form, again making sure that the last comments about you, recited at your funeral, are really what you want said![12] You have been given the unique opportunity to write your own eulogy, so make sure that you incorporate the things that matter the most to you. Did you live and work with meaning? Now, assume that someone else wrote your eulogy. What would be different about it? Remember Scrooge's experience in the classic tale *A Christmas Carol*? What would your encounter with the Ghost of Christmas Future, in which you get a glimpse of your destiny, be like? How would people remember you, talk about you?

Eulogy Exercise

Are you living and working in such a way that the last comments about you, especially from your family, friends, business associates, and customers/clients, are really what you want to have said? Imagine now that you have passed on and have been given the opportunity to write your own eulogy to be read at your funeral. Go ahead, fill in the blanks!

WE HAVE GATHERED HERE TODAY TO SAY FAREWELL TO _____. THE WORLD HAD A GREAT NEED FOR SOMEONE WHO _____ _____ AND _____ WAS THE RIGHT PERSON TO FULFILL THIS NEED.

_____ WAS MOST FULFILLED WHEN _____ _____ _____.

I BELIEVE _____ WAS PUT ON THIS EARTH TO _____ _____ _____.

THE WORLD IS A MUCH BETTER PLACE BECAUSE _____ WAS HERE AND WE WILL MISS HER/HIM FOREVER.

Each of these exercises will not only help you reflect upon your life/work but also detect what is most meaningful to you. In all instances, you are being asked to *step up* in some way (the latter two exercises are more of an out-of-body experience) and see the big picture of your life. You may or may not like what you see. Yet, these exercises also provide you with a chance to consider your life's *ultimate meaning*, as Frankl would say. Irrespective of your religious or spiritual persuasion, ultimate meaning is a metaphysical con-cept, one that clearly has its roots and value in spiritual mat-ters. In his introduction to *The Doctor and the Soul*, Frankl wrote the following: "Life is a task. The religious man differs from the apparently irreligious man only by experiencing his existence not simply as a task, but as a mission." Now ask yourself truthfully: Is your life a task or a mission? What about your work?

As you map your life's path, write your obituary or eulo-gy, draft your personal legacy, or weave together your life quilt, keep these life-affirming questions in mind. By remain-ing aware of the need to detect and learn from the meaning of life's moments, you ensure that you do not become a *pris-oner of your thoughts*. And by focusing on meaning's big pic-ture, your search for ultimate meaning begins but never ends.

Meaning Moment Recall a situation in your work life in which you were forced to deal with the fear of change (this may even be your situation today). Perhaps you were facing a down-sizing or merger. Perhaps you were confronted with a new leadership/management style or the need for job re-training. Or, perhaps you were facing retirement. How did you first come to recognize the fear of change? What, if anything, did you actually *do* about it? As you think about the situation now, what did you *learn* from it? In particular, what did you learn about your ability to confront your fears and respond to change?

 Meaning Question: How is *your* work like a mission rather than a series of tasks?

FOR FURTHER REFLECTION

Imagine that you have written your autobiography—with details about your life and work—and it is now on *The New York Times* bestseller list. What is the *title* of your autobiography? Name and briefly describe the chapters that are in your autobiography. Who are the people included in your Acknowledgements section?

Don't Work Against Yourself

*Ironically enough, in the same way that fear brings to pass
what one is afraid of, likewise a forced intention
makes impossible what one forcibly wishes.*[1]

Have you ever worked so hard at something that the more
you tried the harder the task became and the farther away it
seemed you got from your goal? In other words, one step forward, two steps backward? I know I've experienced this kind
of situation in my life, including my work life. Let me share a
quick example that took place when, as a full-time professor,
I was directing a graduate degree program in public administration at a university in the United States.

Among my duties as director of the academic program,
I was charged with the challenge of obtaining accreditation
from one of the discipline's professional associations. By getting the university on the roster of accredited programs,
which was viewed by those in the field as a prestigious distinction and competitive advantage, my program stood to
gain through increases in student enrollment, faculty

recruitment, research funding, and other embellishments to its resource base.

At the time, I was also a new member of the faculty, so I took on the responsibility of seeking this accreditation milestone as a way of making my mark. I moved full-steam ahead, demonstrating to all that I was totally committed and highly passionate; I was fully convinced that the objective would be reached in short order. The fact that I had been through this same accreditation process before at other institutions, I felt, was sufficient evidence that I knew what I was doing, and my experience would carry me through to another victory.

Alas, this did not turn out to be the case. I found pockets of resistance everywhere I looked, and the more I looked the more resistance I would find. My "expertise" in this process, I learned later, proved to be a liability. In this regard, because I *knew* what to do—and knew how to do it *best*—all of my colleagues were doing it wrong! I became fixated on every detail of the program, and I assured myself that I would be able, single-handedly, to correct any and all imperfections that might jeopardize the objective of gaining full accreditation.

To be sure, I had good intentions, and most of my university colleagues, in hindsight, would probably agree with me. Unfortunately, my fixation on outcome backfired and I was unable to fulfill my ultimate goal; in fact, I never was able to obtain accreditation during my tenure as program head.

Of course, I could easily blame the situation on everyone else or, at least, shift to others the bulk of responsibility for failing to reach my objective. I choose not to do so, however, for I now see how my own actions worked against me. I tried too hard to get everything done "my way" and, as a result, estranged myself from the very colleagues upon whom I depended for success. My fixation on the "right" way to do things, I have since learned, also had the effect of marginalizing their contributions to the process and, in some cases, even invited forms of subtle—if not overt—sabotage. Paradoxically, I had become my own worst enemy and at the time didn't even know it!

The meaning of life *is* meaning. The meaning of life *at work* is meaning. When we look for meaning, there is meaning in the looking. It's right here all around us, within us, and beyond us. But if we try too hard to create meaning, it can often backfire, especially at work. Like our personal lives, our jobs come complete with their own dynamics. But, unlike in our personal relationships, unfortunately we can't always encounter our co-workers with emotional honesty and vulnerability. We think we have to be "professional," we have to have professional goals and accountability. We have to perform.

> *Work usually represents the area in which the individual's uniqueness stands in relation to society and thus acquires meaning and value. This meaning and value, however, is attached to the person's work as a contribution to society, not to the actual occupation as such.*[2]

Sometimes our performance is measurable; what we produce might be immediately tangible—be it in making sales or products, meeting a certain quota in a month, driving a certain distance in a day, meeting a deadline, baking bread, fixing a car, or serving a customer. Other professional responsibilities are less tangible, involving long-term planning and projects that require creative involvement, team-work, complex expectations, and more subjective goal-setting. They all require performance and most often evaluation as well. In our jobs, most of us are accountable to others. We want to please, to perform well, and to be effective at what we do. And it's often when we want to impress others the most that we undermine ourselves. Our thoughts go out beyond our situation; they get obsessed with results and we overlook the very success we are searching for.

Our jobs are always more than our jobs. They represent relationships—to ourselves and to others, to our customers and consumers, to the products we are designing, creating, and selling, to the services we offer, to the environment, and to the way in which what we do has an impact on the world. These relationships weave together through our work, they have meaning individually and collectively. When we focus too intently on outcome, these relationships suffer. The harder we work for success, the more elusive it can become.

> *The job at which one works is not what counts, but rather the manner in which one does the work.*[3]

Having just graduated from college with a degree in business administration, Angela was especially excited when she was promoted to a supervisory position at the drugstore where she worked. It was her first stab at being a manager and she envisioned this promotion as her initial step up the corporate ladder. Of course, she wanted more than anything to do her very best in her new job and prove to her bosses that they had made the right decision to promote her.

Right away, Angela proclaimed her intentions for building better teamwork, sharing responsibilities, and improving performance with all of the employees on her shift. Her enthusiasm appeared to be contagious and it looked as if she would be able to make some major improvements immediately. Since the drugstore was in my neighborhood and I was a regular customer, I had a chance to learn first-hand about the changes that were happening, directly from Angela.

"My co-workers are unbelievably lazy and don't carry their weight around here no matter what I say or do," she openly complained to me one day. I listened and left, assuming that she was just having a bad day. However, this proved not to be the end of the matter. From then on, every time I saw Angela, even if she wasn't complaining directly to me, I would overhear her complain to other customers about her various problems at work. Indeed, she displayed an extremely negative attitude about work and was quick to point out the failings of other employees. In my view, her work situation had become dysfunctional and, from what I could tell, for reasons that were largely her own doing.

You see Angela had been exhibiting two behavioral traits or tendencies—*hyperintention* and *hyperreflection*—that are central to Viktor Frankl's teachings. Let me explain these concepts by using Angela as a case in point. Unbeknownst to her, Angela had begun to micro-manage her employees, with good intentions, in order to attain her goal of demonstrating that she was a good manager and could achieve her stated performance objectives. Unfortunately, she became so fixated on—or obsessed with—accomplishing her mission (i.e., she was "hyper" intending) that she could only see problems (i.e., she was "hyper" reflecting), not solutions to her escalating management dilemma. Paradoxically, the more she complained and called for increased team-work, job sharing, and improved performance the less she was witnessing among her co-workers.

Moreover, Angela had become so consumed with her intended outcome, a form of anticipatory anxiety, that she began to observe herself failing to achieve it, which was evident in her negative attitude about work. In effect, she had created, as so many of us unconsciously do, a kind of self-fulfilling prophecy. Sadly, she was unaware at the time that by letting go of her intentions, she probably would have found ways to resolve the situation and fulfill her original work objectives.

Meaning is found in awareness of the moment, and when we get too far from the moment we start to lose our effectiveness. Even when the stakes are high and our success essential, focusing on the results rather than the process can actually get in the way of a successful outcome. We all know how it works: our nervousness and anxiety about "getting it right" keeps us from getting it right. The higher our expectations about something, the more disconnected we are from the actual accomplishment of it all and the less able we are to participate in its successful unfolding.

Frankl calls this *paradoxical intention*. Our good intentions actually become the cause of our failure. When a specific success is so fervently sought that we overlook and neglect the relationships that are an integral part of the process, we lay the seeds for something to go wrong. We fly in the face of our own success. We neglect our own meaning, the meaning of others, and the meaning of the process.

"My boss is a jerk." "My boss hates me." "My boss steals all the credit." How many times have you made or heard statements like these? Time out. Think about what you are saying, what it really means, and how it may be affecting you or your co-workers. True enough, bosses have flaws and many of them are significant. On the other hand, most bosses are not the pointy-haired characters portrayed in Dilbert cartoons. More often than not, they have moved up in the company for some good reason. So, if you dismiss your boss because of flaws, you may actually be cheating yourself out of a chance to learn and grow.

Again, think about it: What is your boss good at? What can you learn from him or her? What kind of workers get along best with your boss? Are *you* doing anything that brings out the worst in your boss? From the perspective of Frankl's paradoxical intention, are you encouraging your boss, no matter how abusive he or she may be, to be a micro-manager by asking questions every few minutes rather than by doing your job well? And then ask yourself, is that what you really want? If it's not, then it sounds like you are working against yourself!

We are all intuitive; we are all affected by the moods of those around us; we all know feelings of trust and mistrust; we all know when something "just doesn't feel right." We all know when we are being treated badly, or superficially, or carelessly, or dishonestly, whether in our personal life or our professional life. It is the measure of these things that create our relationships, our incentives and motivations to do our best and be our best no matter what the circumstance.

Don't Work Against Yourself

At work, we know when we are being used as part of someone else's agenda. We sense when our intrinsic meaning as a human being is being overlooked in the wake of somebody else's ambition. This is true whether we are a top level CEO or the new kid in the corner cubicle. When someone is so desperate to be recognized at work by a promotion or a raise, there is a sense of artificial behavior at-large. It doesn't feel quite real. Something is missing, and it's usually meaning.

Consider the case of Neal, a software engineer at a major high-tech firm. Newly married, Neal had just completed an MBA degree from a prestigious university and was determined to be promoted to a management position as quickly as possible. Indeed, he was so fixated on showing off his newly acquired management knowledge and skills—primarily as a way to propel himself up the corporate ladder—that he went out of his way to get noticed by his supervisors. Even if it meant ignoring or irritating his co-workers. Although Neal was recognized for his technical skills as a software engineer, this was not the case for his "people" skills. In fact, his co-workers did not consider him a team player, let alone a supervisor or leader, and they voiced their disdain for him whenever possible. At team meetings, during performance reviews, and around the water cooler, Neal, the aspiring manager, was targeted for being out of touch with and disliked by the very colleagues that he had hoped to supervise.

Unfortunately, because Neal was so busy *looking up* at his prospects for promotion, he failed to see that the water was beginning to boil all around him! So, no matter how competent he depicted himself to be as a manager, and no matter how hard he tried to convince his bosses to promote him, he was unable to do so. In fact, he was so fixated on the promotion outcome that the more he tried to get it, the farther out of reach it became! And because Neal was unaware of the meaning moments that seriously begged his attention, he was unable to adjust his course. All things considered, he was working against himself!

Whenever we overlook the opportunity to have respectful and meaningful moments with others at work, we undermine our chances of long-term success. And when we do take the time to nurture our relationships, the definition of success expands exponentially. Our day-to-day, minute-to-minute lives become success in and of themselves; our specific goal-oriented successes become more accessible.

In this regard, it is important to recognize that business issues and personal issues are frequently tied together. "Smart companies know that the individual's ability to create relationships" is the engine that drives value.[4] Trusting each other's motives is also critically important to success, both in the moment and over the long haul. Indeed, if there isn't trust, you get caught up not only in figuring out how others are trying to undermine you but also in calculating how best to respond to their motivations. As a result, the search for meaning at work suffers and the engine that drives value sputters or stalls.

The tendency to hold others, such your co-workers, as "prisoners of your thoughts" can also work in paradoxical fashion to your intentions. For example, in their article entitled, "The Set-Up-To-Fail Syndrome," Jean Francois Manzoni and Jean-Louis Barsoux describe how bosses often consign weaker performers to an "out-group" because they assume that these employees are less willing to go the extra mile, are more passive, and less innovative.[5] As it turns out, this management approach, and the assumptions upon which it is based, become a self-fulfilling prophecy. Because they have been typecast as weak performers and management has low expectations of them, these employees tend to allow their performance to erode to meet expectations. So, even though the bosses sought to get the best performance possible through the out-group assignment, their personal attitudes and business decisions eventually worked against them.

How many of us have been terrorized by a micro-manager? Someone who doesn't have any trust in our ability to be responsible and productive? It is so disconcerting to be treated with such condescension. Often we lower ourselves to the occasion, fulfilling the negative expectations to the absolute best of our ability. Micro-managers, who think their way is the only way, are on a par with missing managers who stay so out of the picture they have no idea what went on to make anything possible. Or how about those managers who profess to practice *Managing By Wandering Around* (MBWA) in the following way: "Keep up the good work, whatever it is, whoever you are!" If the micro-manager, the missing manager, and the pseudo-MBWA manager can just stop long enough to honor the fact that the job *means* something to us; that we *mean* something to them and to ourselves; and that we *mean well*, then progress is possible. If not, we are likely to hover in insecurity and indecision, which doesn't serve us, the manager, or the job.

These three different kinds of managers are seriously

intent on success. But they all overlook the human being right in front of them. In doing so, they reduce their effectiveness on the job and ultimately limit, instead of develop, their success.

For the dignity of man forbids his being himself a means, his becoming a mere instrument of the labor process, being degraded to a means of production. The capacity to work is not everything; it is neither a sufficient nor essential basis for a meaningful life. A man can be capable of working and nevertheless not lead a meaningful life; and another can be incapable of working and nevertheless give his life meaning.[6]

When hyperintentions get in the way of progress, we sidestep meaning. When we sidestep meaning, we undermine relationships. When we undermine relationships, we put respect at risk. When there's not enough respect, there's not enough creativity and productivity. This tendency to set our sights well out beyond our situation, can certainly establish a worthy goal initially. In the process of getting there, however, we have to let meaning lead the way.

And, along the way, we have to trust in our own meaning. Few of us get through our lives unscathed. We get divorced; we lose our jobs, sometimes after many years of dedicated service; our health fails us in some way; our kids fail us; we fail one another. Life can be as full of failures as it is of successes. Yet in our failures we can find tremendous meaning, and only in meaning do our failures have a useful legacy. When our failures become useful we triumph over them. Instead of leading with our disappointment and bitterness over a job loss or a lost relationship, we lead with our ability to have compassion and understanding—for ourselves and for others. Then, in our search for our next job, our next friend, we project wisdom and experience. Our appeal is heightened and our possibilities increase.

It is interesting to note that the power of failure has received an increasing amount of attention in the world of business, both in the literature[7] and among motivational speakers. Management guru Tom Peters, for instance, said recently that "Only with failure can you verify wrong ways of doing things and discard those practices that hinder success."[8] Tales of failure that offer lessons of recovery and fighting back are being used by a new breed of speakers who are turning to the drama of defeat to inspire.

Paradoxical intention is more than a concept; it is a technique that Frankl developed and incorporated into his system of Logotherapy. In brief, the technique of paradoxical intention was used by Frankl as early as 1939 to help patients deal with a broad range of irrational fears and anxieties, as well as obsessive-compulsive behaviors. For example, by asking a patient who suffered from a phobia to *intend*, even if only for a moment, precisely that which he or she feared, Frankl observed dramatic results in reducing the phobia or eliminating it all together. In his words, when used effectively this technique "takes the wind out of the sails of the anxiety by reversing one's attitude and replacing a fear with a paradoxical wish."[9] Indeed, instead of fighting the fear, the person is encouraged to welcome it, even to exaggerate it. In so doing, the person deflates the anxiety associated with the situation by no longer resisting it. Thus, ". . . while anxiety creates the symptoms over and over, paradoxical intention strangles them, over and over."[10]

Let me now describe some situations in which paradoxical intention either was used or may be appropriate. In Frankl's writing, of course, there are many instances in which he used the technique with his patients. Two in particular stand out because they involve a work-related or workplace situation. In one case, the patient was a bookkeeper who was in extreme despair, confessing that he was close to suicide. For some years, he had suffered from writer's cramp, which had become so severe that he was in danger of losing his job. Previous treatments had been of no avail and the patient was now desperate. Frankl recommended to the patient that he do exactly the *opposite* of what he usually had done; namely, instead of trying to write as neatly and legibly as possible (remember, this is before computers), to write with the worst possible scrawl. He was advised to say to himself, "Now I will show people what a good scribbler I am!" And at the moment that he tried to scribble, he was unable to do so. Instead, his handwriting was actually legible. Within forty-eight hours he had freed himself from his writer's cramp, was a happy man again, and was fully able to work.[11]

Another case involved a young physician who consulted Frankl because of his fear of perspiring. In fact, one day he had met his boss on the street and, as he extended his hand in greeting noticed that he was sweating more than usual. This situation was aggravated as the physician's anticipatory anxiety increased with each new encounter. In order to break this vicious cycle, Frankl advised him, in the event that sweating should recur, to resolve deliberately to show people how much he could sweat. A week later he returned to report that whenever he met anyone who triggered his anxiety, he said to himself, "I only sweated out a quart before, but now I'm going to pour at least ten quarts!" The result was, writes Frankl, that the young physician was able, after a single session, to free himself permanently of the phobia from which he had been suffering for four years.[12] And he no longer sweated abnormally when he encountered other people. One could imagine Albert Brooks, in his role as a newscaster in the movie *Network News,* employing paradoxical intention in the memorable scene where he also is plagued with profuse and embarrassing sweating!

In his autobiography, Frankl recalled once using paradoxical intention to get out of a traffic ticket. He had driven through a yellow light and was pulled over by a police officer. As this officer menacingly approached him, Frankl greeted him with a flood of *self-accusations:* "You're right, officer. How could I do such a thing? I have no excuse. I am sure I will never do it again, and this will be a lesson for me. This is certainly a crime that deserves punishment." As the story goes, the officer did his best to calm Frankl; he reassured him that he need not worry—that such a thing could happen to anyone, and that he was sure he would never do it again. The technique worked, and Frankl was saved from getting a ticket![13]

So how might you use the technique of paradoxical intention in your own work and life situations? Basically, you first must be able and willing to shift your attitude about your situation (recall the discussion and exercises covered in Chapter 4). This requires that you "lighten up" (i.e., tap into and rely on your sense of humor) and "let go" in order to see the situation from a different perspective. In short, you need to be ready and able to *plan* for the fear or anxiety to happen rather than fight or ignore it. One exercise you can use to help you with this process, called the Trash Can Exercise, is to first write down and then place your worries, fears, obsessive-compulsive, and/or negative thoughts, into a real trash can or box. By doing this simple exercise, you will find that you have not only effectively identified your worst fears but also have decided to hold them consciously at bay by letting go of them. You can also design, as did Dr. Frankl with his patients, a conscious plan that invites—and *exaggerates*—your worst-case scenarios into your personal life or work life, as the case may be. Without necessarily implementing your "plan," what does it suggest about your situation? What can you learn from it? What might you do with or about it?

> *Paradoxical intention is the exact opposite of persuasion, since it is not suggested that the patient simply suppress his fears (by the rational conviction that they are groundless) but, rather, that he overcome them by exaggerating them!*[14]

Meaning rests in appreciation of the moment, in gratitude, in awareness, and in relationship. When our awareness is only focused on the future, we lose all connection to now, where we are, where others are, and where the meaning is. When we don't appreciate the present, we aren't appreciating the process. When we aren't grateful for the meaning in our life, right now, we aren't honoring ourselves or others.

Our lives are inherent with meaning, no matter how we measure our success. And even when we do reach the pinnacle of professional success in some endeavor, the feelings that come with such success are fleeting. The goal is reached, now what? Suddenly there is a sinking feeling, emptiness settles in, and we wonder what it all really means.

Is this all there is? If we have forsaken the means for the end, then the end really *is* the end!

Anybody who has accomplished a task at great cost to themselves in time, money, or energy will nearly always feel letdown to some degree when it is over. The engagement of our whole being in making something happen gives immediate purpose to our lives, and then it is over. But the more meaning there is in the process, the more deeply satisfied we will feel, no matter what the outcome.

When we treasure the process, the end becomes a new beginning. At work, when we pay attention to those around us, to the integrity of the process, we experience immeasurable success, no matter what the outcome. It is by sustaining the awareness of meaning in our work lives that we sustain the deeper feelings of success. And it is from this relatedness that the other, more specific and intended goal, has the best chance of success.

When we stay true to our personal values in our professional lives, we lay a foundation of meaning. When we work in awareness of the moment, we stay connected to meaning. Our existence, and the existence of all life, is meaning. It is simply waiting to be discovered, whether we work at a construction site, a bakery, a high school, a movie theater, a multinational corporation, a landfill, a restaurant, a home office, or the White House. By not being a *prisoner of our thoughts,* and by not working against ourselves, we bring meaning to work.

Meaning Moment Recall a situation in your work life in which the harder you worked to achieve an outcome the farther away you seemed to be from your goal (this may even be your situation today). You know, the "one step forward, two steps back," kind of situation. Perhaps you were seeking a promotion or were trying to get a creative idea or project approved by your boss. Or perhaps you were trying to finish a project that seemed to have no end. How did you first come to recognize that you were not making progress? How did you rationalize or justify your dilemma? To what extent, if any, did you think or feel that you were partly to blame? To what extent, if any, did you think or feel that you were working against yourself? What, if anything, did you actually *do* about it? As you think about the situation now, what did you *learn* from it? In hindsight, what would you have done differently in this situation?

Meaning Question: How do *you* ensure that you don't work against yourself?

FOR FURTHER REFLECTION

Think about what it means for you to be aware of the connections that you have with your co-workers, including their feelings, and what it means for them to be aware of their connection to you and your feelings. In what way(s) might you strengthen and show that you treasure these connections?

Don't Work Against Yourself

Look at Yourself from a Distance

---

*We know that humor is a paramount way of putting distance
between something and oneself. One might say as well,
that humor helps man rise above his own predicament
by allowing him to look at himself in a more detached way .[1]*

The ad in a London newspaper read "Unemployed. Brilliant
mind offers its services completely free; the survival of the
body must be provided for by adequate salary." Viktor Frankl
quoted this ad in his book *The Doctor and the Soul* to make an
important point about the different ways that people may
respond to being unemployed. To be sure, Frankl was not in
any way suggesting that unemployment is not a serious matter; on the contrary, he emphasizes that being unemployed is
a "tragedy because a job is the only source of livelihood for
most people." By the same token, this newspaper ad reflects
the fact that not all unemployed people experience an *inner
emptiness* due to being unoccupied or to feelings that they
must be useless.

First of all, the fact that we do not have work in the
form of a paid job does not mean that life itself has no mean-

ing for us. Second, our attitude toward any situation, including unemployment and other major life challenges, frames our ability and willingness to respond in a responsible manner. As you can see, the person who placed the ad in the London newspaper turned a dire situation into something humorous because she was able to put some distance between herself and the issue at hand. She was able to look at herself from a distance as well, which, among other things, allowed her to find meaning in her plight and take appropriate action to remedy her situation. Indeed, even the text of the newspaper ad reflects both her sense of humor and her innate, distinctly human, capacity to look at herself in a detached way and rise above her predicament.

If there's one thing I wished I'd learned to do at a ripe young age, it's to laugh at myself more easily and more often. Growing up, I was a very serious person; uptight you might even say. Having a sense of humor, in my early experience, was more likely to get me in trouble—at home, in school, and at work—than it was to help me deal with life's transitions. I didn't learn to fully appreciate my sense of humor until much later in life, but it surely came in handy for me, especially during difficult times, after I found out how to use it effectively.

It might seem contradictory to write about humor in a book about meaning. Frankl believed that, if there is one trait that distinguishes our *humanness*, it's our sense of humor. (We all know dogs who smile—but they don't burst out laughing, especially at themselves, when they forget for the umpteenth time where they buried their latest bone!) Humor about ourselves represents the essence of self-detachment, especially when the joke is on us. It tells us, and anyone within earshot, that we aren't taking ourselves so terribly seriously—and isn't that a relief. Our human ability to laugh at ourselves takes the edge off every serious work situation; and every serious work situation deserves, and needs, a dose of humor. We not only show others that we "don't sweat the small stuff" but we also show ourselves that we're no exception to the principle of self-detachment.

The old joke goes: "Who ever lifted their head off their deathbed to say 'Gee, I wish I'd gone to the office more often.'?" To my knowledge, no one has—so far any way. No matter how meaningful our work is, its meaning comes from our values, the deeper inclinations of our hearts and minds. Our jobs are part of our meaning; they represent our intentions to provide for our families, for ourselves, for our community, and for the world. They aren't *who* we are; they are what we do and how we do it. And when we can joke about what we do, in some way, we take seriously who we are.

An astonishing example of this is the Dalai Lama, the spiritual and temporal leader of the Tibetan people. He has witnessed the most horrific genocide of his beloved people. Millions of Tibetans, including a large number of the spiritual community of Buddhist monks and nuns, have been tortured and murdered by the Chinese. Yet no one laughs louder at himself than the Dalai Lama. Nor do we often see happiness so gloriously displayed. He knows the tragedy of his time, yet he also knows happiness, humor, and lightheartedness.

In their book *The Art of Happiness at Work*, the Dalai Lama's co-author, Howard Cutler, makes the following observation about His Holiness:

Look at Yourself from a Distance

At last things fell into place. I finally understood how the Dalai Lama could claim "I do nothing," as his job description. Of course, I knew that with his lighthearted humor, there was a tongue-in-cheek element to this job description. And behind his joking about doing "nothing," I knew of his natural reluctance, which I have observed on many occasions, to engage in unnecessary self-appraisal. This seemed to grow out of his lack of self-involvement, absence of self-absorption, and lack of concern for how others view his work, as long as he had sincere motivation to be of help to others.[2]

This is a great gift. And when we bring humor to our working world, it too is a gift. Humor is the great equalizer. It makes a CEO less intimidating and a cab driver more adorable, and the other way around. An adorable CEO can do more for morale than a big raise. A funny cab driver can lighten up an entire, responsibility-ridden day (if the driver gets you where you're going on time).

A sense of humor is usually accompanied by cheerfulness. This is another one of those misleading words. Most cheerful people I know have experienced real tragedy in their lives. When tragedy strikes, it takes us to the depths of our grief. Going through grief gets us to cheerfulness. When we know how bad it can be, we find out, as the actor Jack Nicholson would say, how good it can get.

Real cheerfulness is not have-a-nice-day artifice. It's a way of experiencing the present, no matter what the weight of the world or the weather. Cheerfulness celebrates the possibility of meaning around every corner. It buoys us up beyond our individual concerns and invites us and others around us to find something to be happy about. This doesn't mean we hide behind cheerfulness. We simply lighten up and laugh.

Indeed, a moment of humor at the right time can lift us out of our self-imposed misery faster than anything else. When we detach ourselves from ourselves and our situation, we don't diminish the circumstances, we go beyond them. We can see, feel, and appreciate ourselves as separate from the distress. We don't deny; we accept and rise above.

Let's consider some serious topics that have overshadowed corporate America over the last several years: accounting fraud, and the erosion of business ethics. What could possibly be humorous about the corporate crime wave and how could a light-hearted approach be used to possibly improve the situation in the years ahead?

Andy Borowitz, a stand-up comedian and author of the book *Who Moved My Soap? The CEO's Guide to Surviving in Prison*, offers such an approach—one that balances laughter with serious introspection. Speaking at some of the premier business schools in America, Borowitz has shown that satire can be an effective, if offbeat, way to address the subject of CEO and corporate credibility. Getting business ethics into the open and addressing them humorously, in other words, can be therapeutic for both individual business leaders and their organizations. Moreover, Borowitz has already found that his brand of humor can be a useful tool for advancing business education, complementing traditional courses in business ethics. After his presentation at the Wharton School (University of Pennsylvania), for example, one second-year MBA student said "To be able to laugh and find some humor will likely help move us forward. There is still a crisis in how people view corporate leaders." And an incoming MBA student astutely said "It was so

Look at Yourself from a Distance

refreshing. There was an underlying lesson of 'don't take yourself so seriously.'"[3]

People at work don't have to know a lot about the details of our lives; they just have to know a bit about the true meaning in our lives. When we are able to acknowledge our own meaning, we acknowledge the meaning in everyone else's life as well. Then we can detach ourselves from our difficulties, look at ourselves from a distance, and get on with the job, often with humor as our best friend.

In the world of work, emergency medical care workers have considerable experience with a particular kind of self-detachment. In order to be effective, they have to detach from the person whose life they are attempting to save, as well as be able to view themselves doing their lifesaving work in a detached way. Their jobs, by definition, are pressure-filled, stressful, and meaningful. Yet they have to detach themselves from self *and* the situation facing them—often involving the life or death of the person in distress—in order to do their work with meaning. When it comes to humor, on *any* given day a roomful of emergency responders are much funnier than a barrel of stockbrokers on a good day.

Self-detachment allows emergency workers to maintain emotional distance from their patients, so that they don't identify too closely with them during their critical time of need, observing themselves and their work from a distance, so that they may rise above and deal most effectively with the stresses of the moment.

In our post-9/11 country, communities nationwide are responsible for emergency planning for everything from fire and car accidents to bombs and bioterrorism. In one small county (in a Southwestern state) alone, dozens of people will show up at any given monthly meeting. The jobs represented include: police, fire department, emergency medical services, town, county, and state government, environmental groups, Red Cross, Ham Radio, health department, telephone and power companies. For two hours, they discuss the direst of emergency possibilities and how best to respond. There's a laugh a minute—at themselves and one another—along with the serious work that has to be done.

We never know what's really going on in people's personal lives. We do know that they include both challenges and rewards. Some co-workers may go home to isolation and loneliness, others to happy family life. All experience both the joy and grief that life has to offer; they struggle with making ends meet, with teenage kids, with little kids, with no kids, with babysitters, aging parents, car payments, healthcare expenses, and all the other demands of daily life. Every day, people around the world rise to the occasions in their life and go to work. They bring with them their entire lives, even as they focus on the work at hand.

Being able to detach ourselves from mistakes, our own and others, is another skill that's very useful at work. Nobody likes to make mistakes. When we can acknowledge our own mistakes, and laugh at them, it can be a huge relief for those around us. What are mistakes anyway, but lessons to learn from?[4] Who hasn't felt stupid at work, for some reason or another? It comes with the territory. It comes with life. We're only as good as our mistakes. But we have to acknowledge that we made them.

When someone comes to us at work and says "I made a

mistake," most of us feel empathy. It takes self-detachment to own up to a mistake. To look at yourself and say "I goofed" and then move on with your work and life. We are at once the person who doesn't want to make a mistake and the person who made a mistake. The person inside us who doesn't want to make a mistake is in the driver's seat nearly all the time. A mistake is momentary. When we dwell on our mistakes we give them far too much credit. When we acknowledge them and laugh them off, we reassure those around us that their mistakes, too, are momentary and not *who* they are. I'm reminded of a Calvin and Hobbes cartoon in which Calvin trips, flips, and falls down, only to get up with arms outstretched and say, TA-DAAA!!!

Mistakes, of course, come in all shapes and sizes. The big ones might never be fuel for humor, but they are always life lessons. They teach us humility; and eventually, deep down, they teach us meaning. They teach us that we are even more than our most terrible mistakes. If Viktor Frankl could find humor in the concentration camps, perhaps there's no situation imaginable that wouldn't somewhere, at some moment, lend itself to humor.

In his writing and lectures, Frankl described a kind of cabaret that, from time to time, was improvised in the concentration camp. And although this is very difficult to imagine, this form of camp entertainment included songs, poems, jokes, and even stand-up comedy (some with underlying satire regarding the camp) performed by anyone who wanted to. This activity was meaningful, in part, because it helped the prisoners forget their horrific situation, even for only a moment. Frankl reported, "Generally speaking, any pursuit of art in camp was somewhat grotesque. But you might be even more astonished to learn that one could find a sense of humor there as well. *Humor was another of the soul's weapons in the fight for self-preservation*[emphasis added]."[5]

In fact, Frankl trained a friend to develop a sense of humor in one of the camps. He suggested to this friend that they promise each other to invent at least one amusing story daily, and it had to be about some incident that could happen *after* their liberation. One story involved a future dinner engagement, during which Frankl's friend would forget where he was when the soup was served, and beg the hostess to ladle it "from the bottom." This request was significant for, in the camps, only thin watery soup was provided and servings "from the bottom," which were extremely rare, meant that they included peas and therefore would be a special treat!

It's important to distinguish between self-detachment and denial. When we detach, we do so knowingly and with an orientation toward action. We understand our predicament and choose to behave in a way that supports our relationship with others. We might share our burden at work; we might not. But we know what it is and we know what we are doing. On the other hand, denial separates us from our experience and the benefits that can be derived from it. And, when we deny our own experience, we deny the experience of others. Denial leads to disconnection. Self-detachment, on the other hand, leads to connection, learning, and growth.

Frankl frequently employed the technique of self-detachment during his imprisonment in the concentration camps. Indeed, he often kept himself going by imagining himself as an "observer" rather than as a prisoner. Here's how he disclosed to one conference audience how he had used self-detachment for his own survival:

> I repeatedly tried to distance myself from the misery that surrounded me by externalizing it. I remember marching one morning from the camp to the work site, hardly able to bear the hunger, the cold, and the pain of my frozen and festering feet, so swollen from hunger edema and squeezed into my shoes. My situation seemed bleak, even hopeless. Then I imagined that I stood at the lectern in a large, beautiful, warm and bright hall. I was about to give a lecture to an interested audience on, "Psychotherapeutic Experiences in a Concentration Camp" (the actual title that he later used at that conference). In the imaginary lecture I reported the things that I am now living through. Believe me, ladies and gentlemen, at that moment I could not dare to hope that some day it would be my good fortune to actually give such a lecture.[6]

Being able to visualize and use your imagination effectively are two factors that directly support and influence the self-detachment principle. Experience has also shown that self-detachment can be facilitated by immersing yourself in a role (much like an actor) other than yourself. Hence, a useful exercise for practicing self-detachment involves creating a part for yourself in either the movie of your own life or some other movie production in which you must act out a key role.

For example, imagine that you are the principal character in the movie *Defending Your Life*. In Judgment City, they showed video clips of your life's moments of most fear. If you were in Judgment City, what fears would you be confronting and how would you deal with them? How would you justify or defend your actions in the past? It is important to note that your sense of responsibility for discovering personal meaning can be heightened by immersing yourself in such a fictional, yet still autobiographical, detached view of your own life.

In the final analysis, of course, self-detachment is not about detachment at all. While it certainly has been proven to be an effective tool for coping with a wide range of situations, including predicaments and hardships from which you cannot escape, its ultimate value lies in the unlimited potential for bringing wholeness and authentic meaning to life. To summon the power of self-detachment and tap into this potential, however, requires both freedom of thought and a will to meaning. And we can only fulfill these requirements if we are not *prisoners of our thoughts*.

Meaning Moment Recall a situation in your work life from which you felt the need to distance yourself before you could find a proper resolution (this may even be your situation today). Perhaps you were faced with a business decision that wasn't aligned with your personal values or ethics. Perhaps you were thrust into an emergency situation that required swift action. How did you distance or detach yourself from the situation? How did you distance or detach yourself from yourself, so that you could view and review your own attitudes and behaviors? As you think about the situation now, what did you learn from it? In particular, what did you learn about your capacity for self-detachment? In hindsight, what would you have done differently in this situation?

Look at Yourself from a Distance

? **Meaning Question: How do *you* use humor as a way of putting distance between yourself and a challenge at work, instead of getting obsessed with the situation?**

FOR FURTHER
REFLECTION

Think about the ways in which you can help your colleagues and/or co-workers learn and practice self-detachment at work—as a coping mechanism and a tool for learning and growth. What would you have them do to demonstrate that they understand and can apply this principle?

Shift Your Focus of Attention

De-reflection can only be attained to the degree to which
. . . awareness is directed toward positive aspects.[1]

Andy is a former executive with a major software company. He used to make more than $130,000 a year and had a terrific benefit package. He also supervised teams of software programmers in several states and had an office overseas. But no more. Like scores of other well-paid, white-collar workers, Andy lost his job in a lay-off and has been unable to find one that offers the same—or even similar—responsibilities, status, salary, and benefits. Instead, out of desperation, he has found himself grasping at survival jobs offering considerably less.

"Yes, desperate times require desperate measures, " says Andy. He continues, "This is no time to be picky. Since they laid me off, I've sold jewelry in a department store and worked as a cashier at a ski slope, both at $8 an hour. Now I sell golf equipment."

Andy, however, is more than a mere survivor in a job market that calls for such desperate measures. Although he is empathetic, Andy doesn't really see himself as grasping at straws like some other displaced white-collar workers. He would say that he's not in the same boat at all. You see, Andy isn't driven by frustration, money worries, shame, or embarrassment. In fact, Andy doesn't feel that he is going backward; instead, he feels that he's going forward. An avid golfer, he's moved on to jobs related to his hobby—first helping run the pro shop at a local golf course and now selling golf equipment in a mall sports shop. And, in his current job, Andy sees an even more positive side.

"It's a lot simpler and less challenging than it used to be, but I've learned to be humble," he says. "I see guys coming on to the golf course wound pretty tight. They're guys who come in and are late for their tee times and they expect me to do something. I enjoy dealing with people who remind me what I *used* to be like."

Andy has learned a great deal since he was cut from his executive job in late 2001. Among other things, he's been able to see the silver lining in what could have been, for him as it is for so many of his peers, a cloud of despair and a time of inner emptiness. Instead, Andy has shifted his focus to more important matters in his life and has discovered deeper, personal meaning in the process.

> Other things being equal, an unemployed person who maintains his morale will have better chances in the competitive struggle than a person who has become apathetic. He will, for example, be more likely to get a job which both apply for.[2]

There was a voice throughout my childhood that came from inside my head whenever things went wrong. "Think about something else," it said. And I would. I remember once, when I was a teenager, getting thrown by my horse during a jumping competition. I was thrown into a water jump and the horse fell on top of me. Submerged in the water, I recall thinking about whether my horse was all right, whether we would still complete the course, and whether I'd get my homework assignment completed in time for school on Monday morning. I even remember asking myself questions, such as my name, assuring myself that I was still alive if I could answer them correctly!

As kids, we are naturally resilient; nothing keeps us down for long. Our attention spans are short, our interests many, and our involvement with whatever is happening is complete. Most of us knew instinctively how to "think of something else," should someone hurt our feelings, steal our toys, or eat our candy. We might yell and scream for a few moments, but not for long. It wasn't natural to hold on to our thoughts, to become obsessed about wrongdoings. We'd simply get on to the next big adventure. There was always something more exciting to think about.

It's when we're grown up that this skill gets shelved. As adults we learn to think things through, which is useful. But when thinking becomes obsession and we dwell repeatedly upon negative things, it's not so useful anymore. Often it's our work, at which we spend such a large part of our lives, that becomes the scapegoat for our obsessive complaining and negativity. Things are unfair; the boss is a jerk; the co-workers don't cooperate; lunch is too short; the day is too long; the work is too much; the pay is not enough. Sometimes it seems that work exists simply to complain about.

We all know complainers. At one time or another, we've all been one. Sometimes we like them because they do our complaining for us and allow us to vent our frustrations without risk. Other times complainers weigh us down with their misery and we can feel our own moods and energy taking a dive. When we get locked into our own complaining shadow and focus on all the bad stuff, we immediately lose sight of the good stuff. Blaming and complaining get us nowhere, even if we really do have someone to blame or something to complain about. It's time to dust off those old childhood skills, think about something else, and get on with life.

This reminds me of the time I was working in Illinois years ago for the state department of mental health. I was responsible for coordinating social services within a sub-region of the city of Chicago, as well as working with an inpatient psychiatric unit in one of the state's mental health facilities.

This particular facility, along with others in the metropolitan Chicago area, was overcrowded with patients, many of whom were either psychotic or prone to violence, and my unit was suffering from a severe shortage of staff. For these and other reasons, both union and non-union employees complained incessantly about the problems we were facing. Patients, we knew, had a right to treatment in the most humane way possible, and we weren't doing a very good job of providing it. In point of fact, I would say that we were doing a horrible job because we found it almost impossible, under the circumstances, to meet even the most basic standards of care. The facility was so overcrowded with patients that they found themselves sleeping on the floor in the hallways! In short, we weren't even meeting our ethical and moral obligations to care properly for our fellow human beings.

Well, the complaining by staff continued and an increasing number of employees came down with the "blue flu," which meant that they called in sick and made an already bad staffing situation worse. Those of us who were in supervisory or management positions staffed the agency as best we could, frequently working multiple eight-hour shifts. Eventually, the complaining and resistance escalated into a full-blown walk-out and strike led by union officials.

I remember my boss Rita, a registered nurse and long-time mental health administrator, saying "Good for them! However, the show has to go on, so let's see what we can do without them."

Without them?, I thought. How are we going to do that? We're in a serious predicament with no obvious resolution. Maybe she just doesn't get it.

As I now know, that was not the case with Rita. She knew much more than I gave her credit for. For one thing, she focused on the potentially *positive* implications of the walk-out—that we might finally get the resources we had needed for so long. Second, she stressed how much camaraderie was coming into play among those who were left minding the psychiatric unit. We *were* getting to know each other better and, to be sure, relied on each other more than ever. To Rita, our situation reminded her of her medical MASH-type unit in Vietnam. She had survived that situation and she was damn sure that she would do the same this time around. Rita saw in the patients themselves (some of them anyway) the capacity to help *us* out in our time of need. As it turned out, we did find support among the patient ranks and it bonded us in ways that traditional modes of therapy could never do.

By shifting our focus to positive experiences, we were able to find meaning potential in our predicament. Thanks to Rita's guidance and capacity to "de-reflect," as Frankl would say, we were not subdued by our circumstances no matter how dire they appeared to be. Thanks, Rita.

Two things happen when we think good thoughts on the job: we feel better at work and we are better at work. If we use creative distraction when we are upset and frustrated, we open ourselves to constructive action. We see ourselves more fully, more generously; we get out from under our own shadow.

When we are in a miserable job situation, our choices are to either quit or find meaning in what we are doing. Remember, unless you have an armed Nazi guard dictating your every move, you *ultimately* still have the freedom to choose whether to leave or stay in your job. This said, finding meaning sometimes means distracting ourselves from what we don't like. Even when we do love our jobs, we all experience bad, even ugly, days.

When we are stressed at work, we can always conjure someplace else: a favorite place, a favorite activity, sometimes even a favorite smell. One person I know decorates her office with mementos from trips that she has taken around the world. When work gets stressful, she focuses her attention on one of her favorite vacation spots and, in Star Trek fashion, transports herself to it until she feels relaxed. Another person imagines himself going sailing, often using aromatherapy and music to help get him into the spirit of the moment. Whatever works; it could be anything. It's *your* imagination.

Italian film producer and actor Roberto Benigni is known for using his imagination in ways that allow his audiences to go on mental excursions without really going anywhere. In his internationally acclaimed and Academy Award-winning movie *Life is Beautiful*, Benigni shares his sentimental tale about a man trying to shield his son from the horrors of the Holocaust. While the movie has been criticized by those who feel that it unrealistically and inappropriately makes light and pokes fun at something that was so horrific, Benigni's "comedy" was based on the ungainly premise of his father's two-year ordeal in a Nazi labor camp, and therefore is grounded in reality.

The film is the story of Guido, a Jewish waiter who, while imprisoned in a camp, creates and plays an imaginative "game" (you'll have to see the movie to get the rules of this game) with his young son to avoid breaking up and giving up. Unwilling to see his son killed at the hands of the Nazis or demoralized by the horror of their situation, Guido (played by Benigni himself) keeps up his rapid-fire humor and light-hearted, positive outlook in the face of it all.

It has been said, "*Don't sweat the small stuff. And it's all small stuff.*"[3] This is especially true at work. No matter how important we are in the company or organization, in the grand scheme of things, it's the small stuff that makes up our jobs. Most of the time, there's someone else who can do them, which doesn't make our jobs, or us, less meaningful. It means that we should always pay attention to our freedom of imagination: to play, to hike, to cook, to write science fiction, to become president of a small country, which is always available to us. It comes with the territory. To quote Albert Einstein, "Imagination is more important than knowledge."

With the onslaught of television, video games, and the Web, it's easy to forget that we have access to our imaginations at any given moment. We have almost been trained out of using them. But if you talk to anyone who has survived real trauma or has overcome hardship, their imagination is usually their best friend.

In the concentration camps, much like Roberto Benigni's Guido, Frankl seized on various fantasies to fight off ultimate despair. He envisioned meeting his mother once more and visiting with his wife. He also imagined himself climbing mountains again—one of his favorite pastimes. And he fantasized about having a warm bath, and lecturing to a packed auditorium—in this way, he said, his own ambition held him back from final despondency.

For prisoners, it's often food that stimulates their imaginations and sends them off on a mental journey. They recreate, over and over, the meal they will eat when they are free. They can see it, touch it, taste it, and smell it vividly in their mind's eye. It's a meal that sees them through years of isolation and hopelessness. It's a meal that offers meaning to their lives.

When we get too focused on what's right in front of us at work—whether it's an oppressive manager, a wayward employee, a complicated task, or a boring routine—it's like looking at the earth from space and focusing on just one rain cloud over Idaho. We need to remember that life is huge, and so are *our* lives. When we get distressed about our jobs and work, we are losing sight of the meaning in our lives. Our ability to detach from the distress and focus imaginatively on something that pleases us, returns us to our freedom and to our source of authentic meaning.

Creative distraction, or *de-reflection* to use Frankl's word, is also useful when we have to do something really important at work, like give a presentation or be part of a crucial meeting. By calming down and making sure that we are breathing and in our bodies, we can imagine ourselves in a safe and nurturing place. We can fill ourselves with our selves, and not be so vulnerable to whatever role it is we think we are expected to play. When we bring our true, *centered* selves to the situation, even if we don't always "know" the right thing at the right moment, we bring our inherent authority, the person we are, to the situation. This is something to which we are all sensitive. We know when someone is being authentic and we feel comfortable. We like them. We feel at ease. By drawing imaginatively from where we feel most authentic in the world, we can go beyond role playing in our jobs. In turn, an "ethics of authenticity" emerges and real work can begin.[4]

This is particularly important when we think our roles are what people expect. We can often do and say things that enhance our vision of our role at work. But in the long run, it is exhausting—for us and for others. Knowing our job and playing a role are two different things. Being *who* we are and doing our job is the most powerful combination of all.

Sometimes we need help to get there, and it is our ability creatively to de-reflect that can help us the most. It is always available. Just imagine.

Often, when we de-reflect—that is, shift our focus of attention—from what is bothering us at work, we get a different insight into the problem. Many of our challenges with others have to do with how we personally see things, how we make decisions, and the style with which we do our jobs. These can be very different processes for different people. How we constructively perceive these differences can get a big boost from a little de-reflection.

> De-reflection is intended to counteract . . . compulsive inclination to self-observation.[5]

The principle of de-reflection, Frankl would say, helps us to ignore those aspects of our life and work that should be ignored. It also helps to turn us away from being self-absorbed with our problems and directs us towards the true meanings that beg to be discovered by us. In effect, de-reflection encourages us to perceive something new in a situation so that we may let go of our old perceptions and ways of doing. Through this meaning-centered process, we are able to mature by transcending those conditions that limit us, so that we may make new commitments and identify those things that can (and should) be avoided.

Let me introduce you to a simple exercise that can help you practice de-reflection and deal with real, practical issues at work and in your everyday life. It's called the Mental Excursion Exercise. In addition to helping you shift your focus of attention and take a mental journey elsewhere, this exercise can be used to facilitate creative thinking and problem solving.

Begin by jotting on a piece of paper the situation, problem, or predicament you are facing. Now, list *analogous* situations to yours, while making sure that you stretch your imagination as much as possible by deferring judgment. Enjoy the process of free association and making connections in your mind. Remember, you are trying to get away from your problem situation, so identify some situations that are varied and different from each other. As a catalyst and guide, go ahead and fill in the blanks of the following sentence: "My problem situation, *(what is it?)*, is like *(what is analogous to my problem situation?)*." For example, "The challenge of having to merge two different organizations" is like "getting married." Once again, stretch your thinking!

Now, select at least two items from your list of active analogies and brainstorm the things that you would need to do or have in order to resolve each of these situations. In the sample analogy, for example, what are all of the things that you need to do in the process of getting married? Capture your thoughts by listing them. Continue to suspend judgment at this stage of the exercise so that you capture as many thoughts as possible.

Congratulations! You've taken a mental excursion—actually, two or more excursions. Now return to your original issue—your point of departure, so to speak—spend some time generating ideas for possible solutions. The best way to do this step is to make connections between as many of the items as possible on the list and in the original situation. Since you chose situations that were analogous to your original one, you know right away that there is a relationship between them. Your mission, should you decide to accept it, is to use your list of analogous items (for example, the things you identified that need to be done in the process of getting married) as a springboard for generating ideas that may be used to approach, or even solve, your original problem situation (for example, merging two different organizations). Two ideas that might come to mind are: (1) decide where to live (office location) and how to merge two households (offices); and (2) invite the families (executive teams) to a rehearsal party!

We all bring different histories, experiences, skills, and motivations to our jobs. When we incorporate a bit of de-reflection into our processes, we invite others to be as effective as they know how to be without anyone feeling judged by the differences.

Exercising our ability to de-reflect difficulties at work helps us to be more and more resilient. We have a reliable and constructive way of coping when things get difficult. It's a mindset that can serve us in minor challenges, such as deciding what kind of office equipment to buy, and in big ones, such as how to deal with losing our jobs.

In a perfect world, the jobs we love would be ours forever. But more and more skilled people are faced with losing their jobs after many years of employment. Sometimes the shock of job loss is sudden; we are forced into action. Other times we can see it coming—the possibility, if not always the probability. In either case, fear and anxiety come with the insecure territory. It can make us gear up to be better and more impressive or productive employees, or we can shift our focus from our immediate investment in our job and imaginatively look up and out over our personal horizons. The possibilities are unlimited and the choice is ours to make.

Our ability to "forget ourselves" and literally shift our focus of attention can be very useful in the search for meaning. When it helps us reconnect to who we are, who we love, and what's worth doing, de-reflection restores us above and beyond our jobs and our money. No longer a *prisoner of our thoughts*, it restores us to meaning.

(**Meaning Moment**) Recall a situation in your work life from which you felt the need to shift your attention in order to deal with it effectively (this may even be your situation today). Perhaps you were faced with a business problem that was especially stressful. Perhaps you were thrust into an emergency situation that required swift action. How did you shift your focus *from the situation* to something else? What did you imagine, or fanaticize about? What, if anything, did you do as a result of your shift of focus? As you think about the situation now, what did you *learn* from it? In particular, what did you learn about your capacity for de-reflection? In hindsight, what would you have done differently in this situation?

Shift Your Focus of Attention

? Meaning Question: In what ways do *you* use your imagination to shift your focus of attention when dealing with problematic situations at work or in the workplace?

FOR FURTHER
REFLECTION

Think about the ways in which you can help your colleagues and/or co-workers learn and practice de-reflection at work—as a coping mechanism and a tool for learning and growth. What would you have them do to demonstrate that they understand and can apply this principle?

Extend Beyond Yourself

*Don't aim at success—the more you aim at it and make it a target,
the more you are going to miss it. For success, like happiness,
cannot be pursued; it must ensue and it only does so as the
unintended side-effect of one's dedication to a cause greater than
oneself or as the by-product of one's surrender to a person other
than oneself. Happiness must happen, and the same holds
for success: you have to let it happen by not caring about it.[1]*

Andrea Jaeger was the youngest seeded player in Wimbledon history in 1980. At only 15 years old, she was also the youngest U.S. Open semi-finalist that same year. Described as a "pigtailed, teenage Wunderkind," Andrea was positioned for continued athletic success and fame. Yet, by 1984 her career in tennis had come to an end because of injuries and burnout, and Andrea disappeared from the sports radar screen and the public's eye.

Admittedly, the life of Andrea Jaeger had taken a turn, but her legacy was just beginning to unfold. You see, during her years as a tennis phenomenon, Andrea had spent her off time with sick children in hospitals around the world. Through these heartfelt encounters, Andrea's true metamorphosis was taking place. After moving to Aspen, Colorado, in 1989, she made the decision to dedicate her life to terminally ill children, to give them a greater opportunity to experience life.

"The whole mission was to bring opportunities for children with cancer and other life-threatening diseases to enhance their lives and to make things possible on a long-term basis," Jaeger said.

Jaeger created a charity, the Kids Stuff Foundation, and with the help of friends and other supporters, brought children from all over the world to Colorado for a week at a time to experience life outside the hospital room. At first, Andrea relied on local hotels to accommodate her young visitors. However, with the development of the ten acre Silver Lining Ranch, built totally through donations, Andrea's dream for a properly designed facility became a reality. In June 1999 the first children, twenty in all, arrived to stay at the ranch, and Andrea was there to greet them.

The Silver Lining Ranch, which is within the Aspen city limits, touches every soul, in addition to attending to the children's individual needs. Groups are kept small intentionally, and for good reason. "I believe in the philosophy of one child at a time," Jaeger says. She continues: "If you can make a child smile or laugh, well, your place in the world has been preserved. You carry a lot of what the kids bring and, when you see the strength, the character, the hope in their eyes and hearts, it gets you through the darkest hours you could ever have fundraising."

In July, 2001 Andrea Jaeger was interviewed on NBC Dateline. After a tour of the ranch, the interviewer was so impressed, she asked Jaeger "How do want to be remembered?" Without having to think, Andrea Jaeger quickly replied "I don't need to be remembered. I want the *kids* to be remembered." In no small way, Andrea's response shows us that the heart's light within the human spirit is most brightly illuminated when we create meaning *beyond* our own lives.

When we work creatively and productively with others, our experience of meaning can be profound. When we work directly for the good of others, meaning deepens in ways that reward us beyond measure. Whenever we go beyond satisfying our own personal needs, we enter the realm of what Frankl called "ultimate meaning." Some call it connection to a higher self, to God, to our own spirit, to universal consciousness, to love, to the collective good. No matter what it's called, it is deep meaning and it transforms our lives.

We all know team spirit when we feel it, but what exactly is it? A leading authority on team spirit offered the following observation:

When you ask people . . . what it is like being part of a great team, what is most striking is the meaningfulness of the experience. People talk about being part of something larger than themselves, of being connected, of being generative. It becomes quite clear that, for many, their experiences as part of truly great teams stand out as singular periods of life lived to the fullest. Some spend the rest of their lives looking for ways to recapture that spirit.[2]

Team spirit is something that exists among us, almost when we are not looking; it's something we recognize instantly but have difficulty defining. It is bigger than we are, no matter how large our group. Yet it cannot exist without us. And no matter what our goal is, team spirit is not goal oriented. Team spirit comes out of doing and being together. It is part of the process, the results, or "product," always comes later.

It is paradoxical that focusing too much on the goal takes us out of the play and makes the goal more difficult. When team spirit is in place, everything becomes possible. On the playing field, whether in sports or in business, team spirit raises everybody's individual spirits. Even when the result is a smashing success, the personal rewards are always more profound *during* the process. It is the being and doing together that we remember as deeply meaningful and transformative.

What sport, theater, and every job on the planet have in common is the potential for play. When we give and take, when we are there for one another—on the field and off—it's play that brings us together. It gives us rewards that reach beyond our selves and anchors meaning somewhere "out there," where it means something to us all, and beyond us all.

This wonderful manifestation of the human condition is most likely to get squelched where it's needed the most; at work. Being a boss is often like being a parent; we forget everything we learned along the way about play. We forget about fun and games and how well we learn and grow without being told how. Our natural inclination is toward playing together, cooperatively and joyfully. Yet, in the workplace, a lot of managers go into meltdown. Call in the brigades, work is not being taken seriously! Stop the fun before it spreads! Shoot the bastards!

How many of us have had this experience? We're just "getting somewhere" with the task at hand or the problem of the day—whether it's as an individual or part of a group—and we get "caught" having fun. It immediately sucks the creative wind right out of our sails. Spirits get dampened; the progress we've made is tarnished. It's usually only much later, when enough time has passed to allow us to recreate our feelings of success, that progress is restored. If only those beleaguered managers knew what a disservice they are doing to the company when they dampen the spirit of creative play at work. If we aren't getting juiced through working with others, we're getting it from working well as an individual. It's what keeps us at our most productive. It creates exuberance and if we can't freely express it the reward that costs the company nothing is destroyed.

Whenever our work takes us outside ourselves, we experience greater meaning, whether it's doing something as simple as choosing a location for the next company retreat or as complex as creating a meaning-based multinational corporation. When we work to bring meaning to a company, beyond the bottom line, we bring meaning to everyone who works there and to life itself. This is a gargantuan task when it comes to the corporate world because the sole task of a corporation, as a legal entity, is to grow money. Growing *meaning* is not in its job description. But the stockholders, CEOs, and the employees can, if they are heroic, grow meaning in a corporation.

Growing meaning in a corporation takes more than good intentions. Throughout this book, we've seen excellent examples of companies that are focused on things beyond money, where the quest for personal meaning and fulfillment really matters. But what about those companies that espouse such existential values, and yet the rubber never meets the road? I'm not talking about organizations that clearly have no intention of growing meaning. I'm talking about those that say they do.

Years ago, I had the opportunity to work with George, the president and CEO of a mid-sized corporation that specialized in the development of state-of-the-art technologies to promote human potential. Thanks to George's solid reputation in his scientific field, he had worked in the space program, his company was able to recruit some of the best scientists in the country, as well as attract substantial investments of capital. George was flamboyant and charismatic and he loved being in the media spotlight (where he found himself often).

As both a leader and manager, George presented himself as a sort of "guru," having self-published a book that laid out his philosophy of life and business. George saw everyone as interconnected, professing that the whole was greater than the sum of the parts. Moreover, he said that his company was intentionally designed and managed on such principles, presumably to ensure that meaning at work, and meaningful work, would always play a central part of his company. But, even though George talked the talk, and hugged all of his employees—including frequent group hugs—to demonstrate a kind of family solidarity behind his espoused principles, I observed low morale, high turnover, distrust, and disrespect throughout the company's ranks when I was associated with it. It goes to show you: that good intentions aren't enough to grow anything, let alone meaning.

We all know individuals who live beyond themselves

and for others in their work lives and in their personal lives. Usually, they seem to be doing it because it's in their nature, or because they have been blessed with good mentors along their path—including parents, teachers, and bosses, who have guided them by example. I suspect, moreover, that their giving natures often come out of personal experience. Perhaps they suffered as kids and know what it's like, so they become foster parents. Perhaps they were raised with a lot of money and comfort in their lives and want to give back, so they join the Peace Corps. Perhaps they've been to the top of their profession, found it wanting, searched for deeper meaning, and then got a job in a low-paying, nonprofit organization that serves others. Perhaps they've been to the top of their profession, loved it, and been inspired to help others.

If we take just a few minutes to look around in our lives, every day we will see people doing things for others, quietly, unexpectedly, and without compensation. If we were to ask why, they might not have ready answers. But I suspect they would all agree "It feels good." Selflessness feels good. It satisfies something in us that yearns to go beyond or transcend ourselves, that knows we are honoring a deeper meaning in life when we serve the needs of others.

The capacity to extend beyond yourself, according to Frankl, is another one of our unique traits as human beings. Indeed, *self-transcendence*, as it is referred to in Logotherapy, is the essence of our *human*-ness. Put differently, being human basically means relating and being directed to something other than oneself. Recognizing the abstract nature of self-transcendence, Frankl uses the human eye to explain it in a more tangible way:

In a way, your eyes are self-transcendent as well. Just notice that the capacity of the eye to perceive the surrounding world is ironically dependent on its incapacity to perceive itself, except in a mirror. At the moment my eye perceives something of itself, for instance a halo with colors around a light, it perceives its own glaucoma. At the moment I see clouding I perceive my own cataract, something of my own eye. But the healthy eye, the normal eye, doesn't see anything of itself. The seeing capacity is impaired to the very extent to which the eye perceives something of itself.[3]

Although such a comparison with the healthy eye helps us better understand the nature of self-transcendence, another transformational quality may help us come to grips with why self-transcendence is so vitally important. In this regard, there is a humanistic concept advanced in South Africa called Ubuntu,[4] that not only provides the foundation for African management but also is pertinent to our understanding of self-transcendence. The full expression in Zulu of this concept is UBUNTU NGUMUNTU NGABANTU, translated roughly into English as "A person is only a person through other persons." Importantly, Ubuntu is not about relationships per se; rather, it is about human-ness and how only human beings can establish the human-ness of others. This concept is congruent with Frankl's humanistic philosophy. I propose that it is because of Ubuntu (that is, our human-*ness* can only be truly expressed as a "reflection" of others), that self-transcendence occurs. In effect, we must be able to extend *beyond* ourselves so that we can fulfill or realize more *of* ourselves.

To gain an appreciation for the reflective basis for self-transcendence, let me share with you the following story, called "The Echo:"[5]

A son and his father are walking in the mountains. Suddenly, the son falls, hurts himself, and screams: "AAAhhhhhhhhhhh!!!" To his surprise, he hears a voice repeating, somewhere in the mountains: "AAAhhhhhhhhhh!!!" Curious, he yells out: "Who are you?" He receives the answer: "Who are you?" And then he screams to the mountain: "I admire you!" The voice answers: "I admire you!" Angered at the response, he screams: "Coward!" He receives the answer: "Coward!" He looks to his father and asks: "What's going on?" The father smiles and says: "My son, pay attention." Again, the man screams: "You are a champion!" The voice answers: "You are a champion!" The boy is surprised, but does not understand. Then the father explains: "People call this ECHO, but really this is LIFE. It gives you back everything you say or do. Our life is simply a reflection of our actions. If you want more love in the world, create more love in your heart. If you want more competency in your team, improve your own competency. This relationship applies to everything, in all aspects of life. Life will give you back everything you have given to it. Your life is not a coincidence. It's a reflection of you!

Now stop and think for a moment. Are you paying attention and listening to your echo? From what life seems to be calling out to you, what are you calling out to life?

The yearning to be of deep service often comes out of deep suffering. Viktor Frankl, Nelson Mandela, Mahatma Gandhi, the Dalai Lama, Archbishop Desmond Tutu, Aung Sang Suu Chi—all transformed their suffering into service. They experienced their suffering as meaningful in the most profound ways. It wasn't bitterness that resulted from their suffering, it was love—and meaning. The sacredness of being human was the legacy of their suffering and it informed and transformed the rest of their lives. Meaning became their life's work.

We aren't all called to be a Mandela or a Gandhi. But if we pay attention, we will find that life calls to us every day to go beyond our own interests. And, when we do, our own interests are served in ways that are inexplicably and profoundly meaningful. Even when we do the impossible, like forgive.

Getting to forgiveness is perhaps the most challenging thing we can do to go beyond ourselves. At work, this is especially hard because our emotional ties may not be as strong, and therefore neither is the motivation to forgive. Yet when we look at forgiveness in the light of others' ability to forgive, the path should not seem so daunting.

Frankl didn't subscribe to the concept of collective guilt and, whenever possible, fought this idea even though it was unpopular to be against it after the war. He also forgave his Nazi guards; he even felt compassion for them. In his book *Man's Search for Meaning*, he tells the story about the SS officer who was the head of the concentration camp from which he was finally liberated. After his liberation, Frankl learned that this SS man "had secretly spent considerable sums of his own money at the drugstore in the nearby village, purchasing medications for the camp inmates."[6]

Nelson Mandela walked a path of forgiveness during, and after, his thirty years of imprisonment. It almost seems as though meaning holds forgiveness at its core. That we can't get to life's deeper meaning without going through forgiveness—of ourselves and others.

Forgiveness means letting go of our suffering. It has much more to do with our own well-being than that of the person we forgive. When we hold on to our suffering—our resentment, hurt, and anger—we are inside ourselves with self-pity. It becomes a veil through which we see ourselves and others; it becomes something we have to feed, keep alive, and justify. If we don't, we think we allow the other person to be "right" in their unjust treatment of us.

But forgiveness can be one of the most powerful things we do. Like any muscle, it has to be exercised to work well. Forgiveness can be complicated. Sometimes we think it equates to forgetting, diminishing, or condoning the misdeed, but it doesn't. It has much more to do with freeing ourselves from its hold. Our ability to live our lives with love and generosity is impeded when we don't forgive. It doesn't mean that we have to love and be generous to the woman who was disloyal to us at work or the man who belittled our ideas at a staff meeting. It means we forgive them and liberate ourselves from further captivity. Love and generosity will return in their own time.

The search for meaning in our lives takes us on paths large and small. When we go beyond ourselves—whether in forgiveness, unselfishness, thoughtfulness, generosity and understanding toward others—we enter into the spiritual realm of meaning. By giving beyond ourselves, we make our own lives richer. This is a truth long understood at the heart of all meaningful spiritual traditions. It's a mystery than can only be experienced. And when we do experience it, we are in the heart of meaning. We are no longer a prisoner of our thoughts.

Meaning Moment Recall a situation in your work life in which you felt the need to self-transcend, or extend beyond yourself, in order to deal effectively with it (this may even be your situation today). Perhaps you were faced with a perplexing customer issue that required an *extra*ordinary response. Perhaps you were faced with a question of corporate social responsibility that required some soul searching for an answer. How did you extend beyond yourself to deal with the situation? What, if anything, did you do as a result of your shift in consciousness? As you think about the situation now, what did you *learn* from it? In particular, what did you learn about your capacity for self-transcendence? In hindsight, what would you have done differently in this situation?

? **Meaning Question: In what ways do *you* relate and direct to something other than yourself?**

FOR FURTHER
REFLECTION

Think about the ways in which you can help your colleagues and/or co-workers learn and practice self-transcendence at work. What would you have them do to demonstrate that they understand and can apply this principle?

Living and Working with Meaning

*Man's search for meaning is the primary motivation in his life
and not a "secondary rationalization" of instinctual drives.*[1]

"I don't like working with maggots," Rick said to me as we were discussing his current job and career aspirations. Working as a probation officer for the state department of corrections, Rick, believe it or not, was referring to his clients! He had worked in his current position for over four years and had not, he said, changed his views about the people with whom he was in daily contact—people who, obviously, depended on *him* for advice and support.

After some probing, I learned that Rick had grown up as a ward of the state, bouncing between various sets of foster parents with periodic stints in an orphanage. But, rather than becoming sympathetic and compassionate to those in need, Rick's experience resulted in just the opposite outcome—he became insensitive and unforgiving. Unlike many people who have gone through similar situations, Rick couldn't relate (and didn't want to relate) to people who, in his view, weren't able to take care of themselves, who "slurped at the public trough"—that is, who depended on public assistance in some form or another.

After graduation from college with a degree in finance, Rick took the first full-time job that was available. "Anything would be better than busing tables or flipping burgers," he thought to himself. And although he had never imagined working either for government or in a social services position, he jumped at the chance to be a probation officer. Since he needed the full-time work experience anyway, and he figured that he would find something better soon, Rick, the probation officer and human services warrior, came to be.

Right off the bat he knew that this kind of job was not for him. Yet he felt trapped. Working full-time for a regular salary was new to him and he liked it—the regular salary, that is. Plus, the state provided him with a decent benefits package. Most of his friends were envious of him, and Rick soon found himself working on cruise control. He didn't need to feel; he only needed to put in the hours necessary to receive his paycheck and benefits.

When I talked with Rick, he said that he was feeling more depressed than usual, and was having a difficult time getting up in the morning to go to work. During the work day, he said, he felt extremely edgy, complained a lot (about work, his co-workers, his clients), and even looked for things to argue about with his supervisor. He was "cruisin' for a bruisin'" and he knew it. He just didn't know what to do about it. He felt lost, he felt confined, he felt unhappy, and he felt unfulfilled.

Whatever we may say about Rick's psychological makeup, I think that we can all agree with this: Rick is in the wrong job! And, more important, Rick has become a "prisoner of his thoughts." If only he could recognize that he, and nobody else, held the keys to his own freedom.

The keys to unlocking personal meaning at work are, and always have been, within our reach. They are as close as this very moment. Whenever we stop long enough to connect to ourselves, to our environment, to those with whom we work, to the task before us, to the extraordinary interdependence that is always part of our lives, we experience meaning. Meaning is who we are in this world. And it is the world that graces us with meaning.

Yet, it can be through our very own gracelessness that we are graced. And this, too, leads us to meaning, sometimes when we least expect it—through chaos and confusion. Often we lay tracks in our working life that veer off in one direction just as our train of life decides to go in a completely different direction. We are, at those times, a wreck waiting to happen.

Most of us have these times in our lives. The pressures pile on and we adjust and maneuver accordingly. We shift our attitudes, we push our bodies; we reframe our experiences to fit the challenges in our lives. Then something happens and it all falls apart.

When we embrace new possibilities for ourselves, even if they are difficult and challenging, we embrace possibilities for others. And the results can have unanticipated rewards. Viktor Frankl says, "Each of us has his own inner concentration camp. . . . We must deal with, with forgiveness and patience as full human beings; as we are and what we will become."[2]

Life has a way of leading us to meaning—if we let it. And sometimes we have to roll with life's punches. We can be humbled by life's blows and grow in our ability to know deeper and deeper unconditional love for ourselves and others. Or we can toughen up and harden, becoming more resistant and less and less able to love. The choice is ours. And choice, these days, promises to get more and more complex.

There is a saying, "If you want things to stay the same, then something is going to have to change." But if there's one thing that does stay the same, it's change. Our lives, and the world, change more and more rapidly and dramatically as time speeds up with opportunities and possibilities. We are continually challenged to know who we are, what our values are, and how best to live by them. When we take the time to know ourselves, to know and honor our own integrity, we move deeper into meaning. When we act from the center of who we are and what we represent—honesty, fairness, kindness, and love—our lives are in partnership with meaning, on the job and off. To know we are blessed with meaning, that it graces every aspect and every moment of our lives, is true freedom. At work, it frees us from the judgment of our bosses and co-workers; it frees us to be in tune with what we know best—our own melody of life. It's a melody that only we can sing. And when we do, no one can ever sing it for us.

The struggle for existence is a struggle "for" something; it is purposeful, and only in so being is it meaningful and able to bring meaning into life.[3]

When we live and work with meaning, we can choose to make meaning, to see meaning, and to share meaning. We can choose our attitudes to life and work; we can choose how to respond to others, how to respond to our jobs, and how to make the very best of difficult circumstances. We can transcend ourselves and be transformed by meaning. We can find connection to meaning at work, in the most unusual places and with the most unexpected people. Meaning is full of surprises. It defies our expectations and heightens our awareness. It becomes us.

Meaning is also flexible. What makes sense for us at one time in our working lives might not make sense at another time. When we are awake to life's meaning inside us, we too can be flexible. If we are rooted in meaning, we can sway much more flexibly, be it in a breeze or a hurricane.

Our work lives serve us in unique and meaningful ways that only we truly know, understand, and appreciate. Like a fine diamond, our work represents our many facets but it is we who bring light to the work. If our work is fulfilling in and of itself, we know why. If our work serves us in ways beyond the workplace, we know why. It is this "knowing why" that represents meaning. And knowing why means that we know ourselves and what is calling to us at work—whether it's providing financial responsibility to our loved ones, honoring our unique talents, fulfilling the needs of our families, responding to the needs of the world, being available to do the job that fate sends our way, or any combination of the above.

Let's now take a look at our work lives from this "knowing why" perspective. And let's use, as our frame of

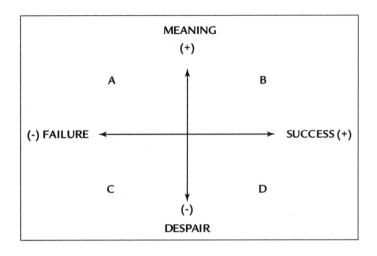

reference, one of Frankl's methods of meaning analysis. The central aim of meaning analysis is to help people "take hold of life" by uncovering and focusing on the core values that, collectively, form the primary motivation in their life, the search for meaning. All human beings, Frankl would say, ultimately have both the freedom and responsibility to position themselves along two key dimensions of life (see the figure above).[4]

One of these dimensions, depicted in the figure as the horizontal axis, suggests that people move between the polar extremes of *success* (+) and *failure* (–) over the course of their lives, including their work lives. The vertical axis, on the other hand, suggests that people also experience different degrees or levels of *meaning* (+) and *despair* (–) over their lifetimes and work lives. Meaning, I should add, refers to fulfilling or realizing the person's will to meaning; despair is associated with the apparent meaninglessness of life.

So, how do we use the figure, which, thanks to Viktor

Frankl, provides us with a visual interpretation of our existential stand, and what does it tell us? First, for illustration purposes, let's consider the kinds of people who, in light of their situation, might be placed in any of the four quadrants or along either of the two axes. For example, a wealthy and successful business executive, who nevertheless may view work as unfulfilling and/or life as devoid of meaning, would be represented by a point somewhere in quadrant D. Think now of people who might also fall in this category—perhaps highly successful in a traditional, material sense, yet unfulfilled, suffering from despair and inner emptiness. We all know, or know of, these quadrant D people, don't we? Not only corporate icons or celebrities or star athletes but also our co-workers, bosses, friends, neighbors, and family members. Think about it.

On the other hand, consider the people who could hardly be considered successful by societal standards—they may exist modestly on a meager salary or pension—but who may be fully content and happy with their work and everyday life. They may be working in a low-paying, low-profile job or volunteering namelessly for a nonprofit cause. In the figure, we would find these people somewhere in quadrant A. Who might you place in this quadrant?

Quadrant B of the figure presents possibilities for identifying people who are *both* successful in a societal sense and fulfilled in a meaning sense. You may recall the story of Tom Chappell and how he effectively moved along the vertical axis towards meaning while remaining on the success side of the horizontal dimension. And don't forget the remarkable and inspirational life of Christopher Reeve. There are others who exhibit the traits of a quadrant B life: from the business world, from sports (remember Andrea Jaeger?), from government and politics—indeed, from all sectors of our society.

You get the picture. The figure, in essence, is a diagram of life. But what about *your* life? What about *your* work? Where would you place yourself in this two-dimensional space? And where, you should ask yourself, would you *like* to be? In a 1953 letter, Frankl wrote, "It is said: where there is a will, there is a way; I add, where there is an aim, there is a will." Do you have the kind of will that Frankl is referring to? Do you also have an aim? Where does it appear to be taking you, not just on the horizontal axis but along the vertical axis as well? What does work mean to you and what *kind* of work really matters to you?

Imagine now a job or kind of work that you really want to do. Ask yourself: Would this kind of work help me realize my will to meaning? If so, what do I have to do to get the job? What am I doing now that will help me along the way? What am I doing now that *is* in my way? What *can* I do now that will help me along the way?

No matter what our specific job might be, it is the *work* we do that represents who we are. When we meet our work with enthusiasm, appreciation, generosity, and integrity, we meet it with meaning. And no matter how mundane a job might seem at the time, we can transform it with meaning. Meaning is life's legacy, and it is as available to us at work as it is available to us in our deepest spiritual quests. We breathe, therefore we are—spiritual. Life is; therefore it is—meaningful. We do, therefore we work.

Viktor Frankl's legacy was one of hope and possibility. He saw the human condition at its worst, and human beings behaving in ways intolerable to the imagination. He also saw human beings rising to heights of compassion and caring in ways that can only be described as miraculous acts of unselfishness and transcendence. There is something in us that can rise above and beyond everything we think possible. Our instinct for meaning, in our work and in our everyday lives, is ours right now, at this very moment. As long as we are not a prisoner of our thoughts.

> *We must never be content with what has already been achieved. Life never ceases to put new questions to us, never permits us to come to rest. . . .The man who stands still is passed by; the man who is smugly contented loses himself. Neither in creating or experiencing may we rest content with achievement; every day, every hour makes new deeds necessary and new experiences possible.*[5]

Meaning Moment   Recall a situation in your work life in which you felt trapped or confined in some way and didn't feel fulfilled (this may even be your situation today). Perhaps you were working in a job or position that you really didn't like. Perhaps you were doing work that didn't seem meaningful to you. What, if anything, did you do about this situation? Did you resolve it or did it resolve itself? As you think about the situation now, what did you *learn* from it? In hindsight, what would you have done differently in this situation?

Meaning Question: In what ways do *you* find meaning and fulfillment at work?

Think about the ways in which you can help your colleagues and/or co-workers unlock personal meaning and fulfillment in their work. What would you have them do to demonstrate that they understand their responsibility to "stand up" to life and work, in order to find personal meaning and fulfillment?

Notes

CHAPTER 1

1. Viktor E. Frankl, *Man's Search for Meaning: An Introduction to Logotherapy* (Boston: Beacon Press, 4th Edition, 1992), pp. 113–14.
2. Viktor E. Frankl, *Psychotherapy and Existentialism* (New York: Washington Square Press, 1967), p. 122.
3. Viktor E. Frankl, *Viktor Frankl Recollections: An Autobiography* (New York: Plenum Press, 1997), p. 53.
4. Personal conversation, Vienna, Austria, August 6, 1996. *See also* Viktor E. Frankl, keynote address, Evolution of Psychotherapy Conference, Anaheim, California, December 12–16, 1990.
5. See Deepak Chopra, *Unconditional Life: Discovering the Power to Fulfill Your Dreams* (New York: Bantam Books, 1991).
6. Viktor E. Frankl, *The Unheard Cry for Meaning* (New York: Washington Square Press, 1978), p. 45.
7. Stephen R. Covey, *The 7 Habits of Highly Effective People* (New York: Simon & Schuster, 1989), p. 277.
8. Viktor E. Frankl, *The Will to Meaning*, 1985 lecture, available on tape from Zeig, Tucker & Theisen, Publishers, Phoenix, Arizona, ISBN: 1-932462-08-2; See also Viktor E. Frankl, *The Will to Meaning: Foundations and Applications of Logotherapy* (New York: Penguin Books, 1988).
9. Viktor E. Frankl, *The Unconscious God* (New York: Washington Square Press, 1975), p. 120.
10. Frankl, *Man's Search for Meaning*, p. 75.
11. Frankl, *Man's Search for Meaning*, p. 108.
12. Frankl, *Man's Search for Meaning*, p. 49.
13. Viktor E. Frankl, lecture, Religion in Education Foundation, University of Illinois, February 18, 1963. *See also* Viktor E. Frankl, *Psychology and Existentialism*, p. 147.
14. Frankl, *Psychotherapy and Existentialism*, p. 4.

CHAPTER 2

1. Viktor E. Frankl, *Viktor Frankl Recollections: An Autobiography* (New York: Plenum Press, 1997), p. 35.
2. Frankl, *Viktor Frankl Recollections: An Autobiography*, p. 19.
3. Frankl, *Viktor Frankl Recollections: An Autobiography*, p. 53.
4. Frankl, *Viktor Frankl Recollections: An Autobiography*, p. 98.
5. Frankl, *Viktor Frankl Recollections: An Autobiography*, p. 53.
6. Viktor E. Frankl, *Man's Search for Meaning: An Introduction to Logotherapy* (Boston: Beacon Press, 4th Edition, 1992), pp. 147–49.
7. See also Frankl, *Man's Search for Meaning*, p. 117.
8. Frankl, *Man's Search for Meaning*, p 75.
9. Stephen R. Covey, A. Roger Merrill, and Rebecca R. Merrill, *First Things First* (New York: Simon & Schuster, 1995), p. 103.

CHAPTER 3

1. Viktor E. Frankl, *Man's Search for Meaning: An Introduction to Logotherapy* (Boston: Beacon Press, 4th Edition, 1992), p. 115.

CHAPTER 4

1. Viktor E. Frankl, *Man's Search for Meaning: An Introduction to Logotherapy* (Boston: Beacon Press, 4th Edition, 1992), p 75.
2. I am indebted to Dr. Myron S. Augsburger for this account. See also: Nelson Mandela, *Long Walk to Freedom* (New York: Little, Brown and Company, 1995).
3. Christopher Reeve, *Still Me* (New York: Ballantine Books, 1999). p. 267.
4. *Larry King Live*, February 22, 1996.
5. Reeve, *Still Me*, pp. 3–4.
6. See: Christopher Reeve, *Nothing is Impossible: Reflections on a New Life* (New York: Random House, 2002).
7. Frankl, keynote address, Evolution of Psychotherapy Conference, Anaheim, California, December 12–16, 1990.
8. Viktor E. Frankl, *Psychotherapy and Existentialism* (New York: Washington Square Press, 1967), p. 3.

CHAPTER 5

1. Viktor E. Frankl, *Man's Search for Meaning: An Introduction to Logotherapy* (Boston: Beacon Press, 4th Edition, 1992), pp. 87–88.
2. See, for example: www.thestackeddeck.com; www.wallstreetmost-wanted.com.

3. David Packard, *The HP Way* (New York: HarperCollins Publishers, 1995), p. 82.

4. Ann Kerr, "Workers Spurn Retirement," *The Globe and Mail*, February 18, 2002.

5. Rodney Crowell, "Time to Go Inward" (track 4), from the album, *Fate's Right Hand*, New York: Sony Music Entertainment, Inc., 2003. Note: I'm indebted to my friend and colleague Stewart Levine, for introducing me to Rodney Crowell's music and lyrics.

6. Viktor E. Frankl, *The Unheard Cry for Meaning* (New York: Washington Square Press, 1978), p. 21.

7. Kalle Lasn and Bruce Grierson, "America the Blue", *Utne Reader On-Line*, October 28, 2000.

8. See Dan Pink, *Free Agent Nation: How America's New Independent Workers Are Transforming the Way We Live* (New York: Warner Books, 2001).

9. TGIF is an acronym for "Thank God It's Friday."

10. Thomas Moore, *The Re-Enchantment of Everyday Life* (New York: HarperCollins, 1996), p. 126.

11. In Roger Frantz and Alex Pattakos, eds., *Intuition at Work: Pathways to Unlimited Possibilities* (San Francisco: New Leaders Press, 1996), p. 4.

12. Frankl, *Man's Search for Meaning*, p. 49.

13. Moore, *The Re-Enchantment of Everyday Life*, p. 11.

CHAPTER 6

1. Viktor E. Frankl, *Man's Search for Meaning: An Introduction to Logotherapy* (Boston: Beacon Press, 4th Edition, 1992), p. 114.

2. Frankl, *Man's Search for Meaning*, p. 115.

3. See, for example, Phil Jackson and Hugh Delehanty, *Sacred Hoops: Spiritual Lessons of a Hardwood Warrior* (New York: Hyperion, 1995).

4. Viktor E. Frankl, keynote address, Evolution of Psychotherapy Conference, Anaheim, California, December 12–16, 1990.

5. Frankl, *Man's Search for Meaning*, p. 107.

6. Viktor E. Frankl, *The Doctor and the Soul: From Psychotherapy to Logotherapy* (New York: Random House, 1986), p. xix.

7. Kathleen D. Ryan and Daniel K. Oestreich, *Driving Fear Out of the Workplace: Creating the High-Trust, High-Performance Organization* (San Francisco: Jossey-Bass, 1998).

8. See, for example: Susan Jeffers, *Feel the Fear and Do It Anyway* (New

York: Ballantine Books, 1988); and Alan Downs, *The Fearless Executive* (New York: AMACOM Books, 2000).

9. Frankl, *Man's Search for Meaning*, p. 135.
10. Mark Gerzon, *Coming Into Our Own: Understanding the Adult Metamorphosis* (New York: Delacorte Press, 1992).
11. See Frankl, *The Doctor and the Soul*, p. 26.
12. I'm indebted to Art Jackson for introducing me to this particular exercise.

CHAPTER 7

1. Viktor E. Frankl, *Man's Search for Meaning: An Introduction to Logotherapy* (Boston: Beacon Press, 4th Edition, 1992), p. 125.
2. Viktor E. Frankl, *The Doctor and the Soul: From Psychotherapy to Logotherapy* (New York: Random House, 1986), p. 118.
3. Frankl, *The Doctor and the Soul*, p. 118.
4. See: Ronna Lichtenberg, *It's Not Business, It's Personal: The 9 Relationship Principles That Power Career* (New York: Hyperion, 2002).
5. Jean Francois Manzoni and Jean-Louis Barsoux, "The Set-Up-To-Fail Syndrome," *Harvard Business Review*, March-April 1998, pp. 101–113.
6. Frankl, *The Doctor and the Soul*, p. 126.
7. See, for example: Charles C. Manz, *The Power of Failure* (San Francisco: Berrett-Koehler Publishers, 2002).
8. Robert Johnson, "Speakers Use Failure to Succeed," *The Globe and Mail*, January 30, 2001, p. B16A.
9. Frankl, *The Doctor and the Soul*, p. 224.
10. Haddon Klingberg, *When Life Calls Out to Us: The Love and Lifework of Viktor and Elly Frankl* (New York: Doubleday, 2001), p. 67; See also: Frankl, *The Doctor and the Soul*, p. 232.
11. Frankl, *Man's Search for Meaning*, p. 128.
12. Frankl, *Man's Search for Meaning*, p. 127.
13. Frankl, *Viktor Frankl Recollections: An Autobiography*, pp. 67–68.
14. Frankl, *The Doctor and the Soul*, p. 224.

CHAPTER 8

1. Viktor E. Frankl, *Psychotherapy and Existentialism* (New York: Washington Square Press, 1967),
2. The Dalai Lama and Howard C. Cutler, *The Art of Happiness at Work* (New York: Riverhead Books, 2003), p. 200.
3. *USA Today*, August 19, 2003, pp. 1B–2B.

4. Charlotte Foltz Jones, *Mistakes That Worked* (New York: Delacorte Press, 1991).
5. Rubin Battino, *Meaning: A Play Based on the Life of Viktor E. Frankl* (Williston, Vermont: Crown House Publishing Limited, 2002), p. 66; See also: Frankl, *Man's Search for Meaning*, p. 54.
6. Viktor E. Frankl, *Viktor Frankl Recollections: An Autobiography*, p. 98; See also Frankl, keynote address, Evolution of Psychotherapy Conference, Anaheim, California, December 12–16, 1990; Frankl, *Man's Search for Meaning*, pp. 81–82.

CHAPTER 9

1. Viktor E. Frankl, *The Doctor and the Soul: From Psychotherapy to Logotherapy* (New York: Random House, 1986), p. 254.
2. Frankl, *The Doctor and the Soul*, p. 125.
3. See Robert Carlson, *Don't Sweat the Small Stuff at Work* (New York: Hyperion, 1999).
4. See Charles Taylor, *The Ethics of Authenticity* (Cambridge, Massachusetts: Harvard University Press, 1991).
5. Frankl, *The Doctor and the Soul*, p. 255.

CHAPTER 10

1. Viktor E. Frankl, *Man's Search for Meaning: An Introduction to Logotherapy* (Boston: Beacon Press, 4th Edition, 1992), p. 12.
2. Peter M. Senge, *The Fifth Discipline* (New York: Currency/Doubleday, 1994), p. 13.
3. Klingberg, *When Life Calls Out to Us: The Love and Lifework of Viktor and Elly Frankl*, p. 289. Speech given before Toronto Youth Corps, February 11, 1973.
4. Lovemore Mbigi and Jenny Maree, *Ubuntu: The Spirit of African Transformation Management* (Randburg, South Africa: Knowledge Resources Ltd., 1997).
5. Source unknown; See: Elaine Dundon and Alex Pattakos, *Seeds of Innovation Insights Journal, Volume One* (Santa Fe, New Mexico: The Innovation Group, 2003), p. 41.
6. Frankl, *Man's Search for Meaning*, pp. 92–93.

CHAPTER 11

1. Viktor E. Frankl, *Man's Search for Meaning: An Introduction to Logotherapy* (Boston: Beacon Press, 4th Edition, 1992), p. 105.
2. Personal conversation, Vienna, Austria, August 6, 1996; See also:

Frankl, keynote address, Evolution of Psychotherapy Conference, Anaheim, California, December 12–16, 1990.

3. Frankl, *The Will to Meaning*, 1985 lecture, available on tape from Zeig, Tucker & Theisen, Publishers, Phoenix, Arizona, ISBN: 1-932462-08-2; See also *The Will to Meaning: Foundations and Applications of Logotherapy* (New York: Penguin Books, 1988).

4. Viktor E. Frankl, *Psychotherapy and Existentialism* (New York: Washington Square Press, 1967), p. 27.

5. Viktor E. Frankl, *The Doctor and the Soul: From Psychotherapy to Logotherapy* (New York: Random House, 1986), p. 130–31.

References

Albion, Mark. (2000). *Making a Life: Reclaiming Your Purpose and Passion in Business and in Life*. New York: Warner Books.

Battino, Rubin. (2002). *Meaning: A Play Based on the Life of Viktor Frankl*. Williston, Vermont: Crown House Publishing Limited.

Bulka, Reuven P. (1979). *The Quest for Ultimate Meaning: Principles and Applications of Logotherapy*. New York: Philosophical Library.

Coetzer, Patti Havenga. (2003). *Viktor Frankl's Avenues to Meaning: A Compendium of Concepts, Phrases and Terms in Logotherapy*. Benmore, South Africa: Viktor Frankl Foundation of South Africa.

Covey, Stephen R. (1989). *The 7 Habits of Highly Effective People*. New York: Simon & Schuster.

Covey, Stephen R., Merrill, A. Roger, and Merrill, Rebecca R. (1994). *First Things First: To Live, to Love, to Learn, to Leave a Legacy*. New York: Simon & Schuster.

Fabry, Joseph B. (1968). *The Pursuit of Meaning: Logotherapy Applied to Life*. Boston: Beacon Press.

Fabry, Joseph B., Bulka, Reuven P., and Sahakian, William S. Eds. (1995). *Finding Meaning in Life: Logotherapy*. Northvale, New Jersey: Jason Aronson Inc.

Frankl, Viktor E. (1967). *Psychotherapy and Existentialism*. New York: Simon & Schuster.

Frankl, Viktor E. (1978). *The Unheard Cry for Meaning*. New York: Washington Square Press.

Frankl, Viktor E. (1986). *The Doctor and the Soul: From Psychotherapy to Logotherapy*. New York: Vintage Books.

Frankl, Viktor E. (1988). *The Will to Meaning: Foundations and Applications of Logotherapy*. New York: New American Library.

Frankl, Viktor E. (1992). *Man's Search for Meaning*, 4th ed. Boston: Beacon Press.

Frankl, Viktor E. (1997). *Man's Search for Ultimate Meaning*. New York: Plenum Press.

Frankl, Viktor E. (1997). *Viktor Frankl Recollections: An Autobiography.* New York: Plenum Press.

Gill, Ajaipal Singh. (2000). *Frankl's Logotherapy and the Struggle Within.* Pittsburgh: Dorrance Publishing Co., Inc.

Gould, William Blair. (1993). *Frankl: Life With Meaning.* Pacific Grove, CA: Brooks/Cole Publishing Company.

Graber, Ann V. (2003). *Viktor Frankl's Logotherapy: Method of Choice in Ecumenical Pastoral Psychology.* Lima, OH: Wyndham Hall Press.

Klingberg, Haddon (2001). *When Life Calls Out to Us: The Love and Life-work of Viktor and Elly Frankl.* New York: Doubleday.

Lasn, Kalle, and Grierson, Bruce. (2000). "America the Blue." *Utne Reader On-Line.* October 28.

Martin, Mike W. (2000). *Meaningful Work.* New York: Oxford University Press.

McCain, John. (1999). *Faith of My Fathers.* New York: Random House.

Morgan, John H. (1987). *From Freud to Frankl: Our Modern Search for Personal Meaning.* Bristol, IN: Wyndham Hall Press.

Naylor, Thomas H., Willimon, William H., and Naylor, Magdaelena R. (1994). *The Search for Meaning.* Nashville, TN: Abingdon Press.

Taylor, Charles. (1991). *The Ethics of Authenticity.* Cambridge: Harvard University Press.

Tengan, Andrew. (1999). *Search for Meaning as the Basic Human Motivation.* Frankfurt, Germany: Peter Lang.

Terez, Tom. (2000). *22 Keys to Creating a Meaningful Workplace.* Holbrook, MA: Adams Media Corporation.

Wong, Paul T. P., and Prem S. Fry (1998). *The Human Quest for Meaning.* Mahwah, NJ: Lawrence Erlbaum.

Index

Care of the Soul (Moore), 14
career, giving meaning to a, 2
cartoon, Calvin and Hobbes, 124
case histories
   accreditation application,
      99–101
   American diplomat in Vienna,
      86–87
   Andrea Jaeger, 143–145
   Andy, software company execu-
      tive, 129–130
   Angela, new drugstore manager,
      102–104
   Bob, financial services executive,
      34–35
   bookkeeper with writers cramp,
      111
   Charlotte, dealing with an autis-
      tic son, 62–63
   Frankl's personal application of
      paradoxical intention, 112
   General Stylianos Pattakos,
      political prisoner, 39–41
   George, difficulty of ensuring
      meaning at work, 148
   Jerry Long, accident victim,
      22–23
   Kate and Tom Chappell, Tom's
      of Maine, 30–33
   Michelle, stressful job situations,
      79–80
   Neal, software engineer, 106–107
   Paul, U.S. Forest Service, 53–54
   physician with fear of perspiring,
      111–112
   Rebecca, creativity consultant,
      48–49
   Rick, probation officer, 155–157
   Rita, mental health care admin-

istrator, 132–134
   Tom, former high-tech worker,
      47–48
   traffic accident incident, 50–52
   Vita, mail carrier, 1–3
   Winston, bus driver, 28–29, 33
catastrophe
   attitude towards, 50–52
   coping with, 43
cell phones, addiction to, 84
challenges, attitude towards life,
   118
change
   nature of, 158
   results of organizational, 47–48
Chappell, Kate, Tom's of Maine,
   30–33
Chappell, Tom, Tom's of Maine,
   30–33, 70
charity, Andrea Jaeger's Kids Stuff
   Foundation, 144–145
Chartres Cathedral, the labyrinth
   in, 26
cheerfulness, grief, 120
choice
   meaning, 4
   quit or find meaning, 134–135
Chopra, Deepak, *Unconditional
   Life*, 4
Clearlake, Tom's of Maine, 30
Clinton, Bill, and Nelson Mandela, 40–41
club, "bitch and moan", 35
*Coming Into Our Own: Under-
   standing the Adult Metamorphosis* (Gerzon), 91
communication, changes in,
   83–84
communities, Buddhist, 64

Kristofferson, Kris, 65

labyrniths, of meaning, 25–37
Laing, R.D., our personal limitations, xii
Larry King Live, Christopher Reeve interview, 42–43
Lay, Ken, Enron, 58
legacy, personal, 93
Les Miserables (Hugo), Jean Valjean in, 34–35
lessons, mistakes and life, 124
liberation, forgiveness, 153
life
    creative expansion of, 47–49
    flexibility, 159
    out of balance, 14
    retirement from vs. redesign of, 92–93
    rolling with the punches, 158
    task vs. mission, 96
    "The Echo", 150–151
    Viktor Frankl on, xiii
    Viktor Frankl's, xv-xviii, 17–22
Life is Beautiful, Roberto Benigni as Guido in, 135
lists, ten positive things, 49–54
living
    from the inside out, 65
    for the second time, 79
Logotherapy
    development of, 69
    goal of, 6–7
    paradoxical intention, 110–113
    psychotherapy approach, xv–xvi
    self-transcendence, 149–150
Long, Jerry, 22–23
love
    essence of mortality, x

ultimate goal, 88
work, 9

Malden Mills, fire at, 74–75
man, salvation of, 73–74
management, styles of, 108–109
Mandela, Nelson
    forgiveness, 152
    President Bill Clinton, 40–41
Man's Search for Meaning (Frankl)
    concentration camp experience, 20–21
    human freedoms, 9
    Logotherapy, xv
    soul's code, viii
    manuscript, *The Doctor and the Soul*, 20
Manzoni, Jean Francois and Jean-Louis Barsoux, "The Set-Up-To-Fail-Syndrome", 107–108
map, your life, 93–94
Maslow, Abraham, *The Farther Reaches of Human Nature*, x–xi
maxim, coping, 45–46
MBWA (Managing By Wandering Around), 108–109
McCain, John, *Faith of My Fathers*, 23
meaning
    analysis grid, 160–162
    continual search for, 7–11
    filling a void of, 58
    finding, 4
    Frankl's legacy of, 22–24
    growing in a corporation, 147–148
    search for, 80–82
    unheard cry for, 71
    will to, 7, 58–59

About the Author

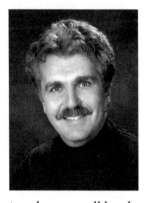

Alex Pattakos, Ph.D., is a principal of The Innovation Group (www.seedsofinnovation.com), and founder of the Center for Personal Meaning, based in Santa Fe, New Mexico, USA. He is well known for his high energy, inspiration, and dynamic approach to engaging participants and effecting change at all levels. As a speaker, author, facilitator, consultant, he brings his unique perspective and experience base to help clients re-energize and identify new approaches to planning their futures. As a personal counselor and coach, he works closely with executives, athletes, celebrities, workers from all sectors, and retirees to help them find meaning in their work and everyday lives.

Dr. Pattakos also has over twenty-five years experience with "community building" in a wide variety of settings—business, government, and nonprofit. He has worked extensively with organizations at all levels to advance their capacities in innovative decision making, organizational learning, leadership development, and systems redesign. His corporate clients include those on the Fortune 500 across a wide variety of industries. He also serves as an adviser to governments at the federal, state/provincial, and local levels on public policy and management matters. In this regard, Dr. Pattakos was one of the initial faculty evaluators for the Innovations in American Government Awards Program at the John F. Kennedy School of Government, Harvard University. He is a pioneer in the innovative use of technology to enhance individual and group learning and is credited by the World Futures Society as the inventor of the "Electronic Visiting Professor" concept, an innovation in online distance learning when the Information Highway was still a dirt road. His work in this area has been shared internationally through the Voice of America and his perspective on "creative learning" can be found in his contributions to the book, *Managing in Organizations that Learn.* Dr. Pattakos believes that innovation must be viewed holistically, that it is a collaborative enterprise, and that everyone is innovative and can learn to be more innovative.

As a past president of Renaissance Business Associates (RBA), a nonprofit, international association of people committed to integrity in business and elevating the human spirit in the workplace, Dr. Pattakos worked to advance spiritual and ethical approaches to public policy development and corporate/business management. During his tenure, RBA was active in Australia, Canada, Europe, Nigeria, South Africa, and the USA.

Among his other publications, he is the co-editor/co-author of the book, *Intuition at Work: Pathways to Unlimited Possibilities,* and a contributing author of the book, *Rediscovering the Soul of Business: A Renaissance of Values.* His work to enhance the creative spirit in organizations has been featured in *Executive Excellence, Success, Personnel Journal, Training,* and *Investors' Business Daily* magazines, among others.

An avid martial artist and thespian, Dr. Pattakos seeks to integrate the philosophy and techniques from both experiences into his public speaking and other engagements.

For further information:
The Innovation Group
223 North Guadalupe Street, #243
Santa Fe, New Mexico 87501-1850 USA
Office: (505) 820-0254
e-mail: info@prisonersofourthoughts.com
www.prisonersofourthoughts.com

Please see next pages for other books
from Berrett-Koehler Publishers

Answering Your Call
A Guide for Living Your Deepest Purpose

John P. Schuster

Answering Your Call doesn't just show how to discover your calling, but how to hear it, how to respond to it, and how to make it a reality in your life. John P. Schuster provides practical advice and useful exercises that will help you on your way to doing what you are meant to do.

Paperback • ISBN 1-57675-205-4 • Item #52054 $15.95

The Power of Purpose
Creating Meaning in Your Life and Work

Richard J. Leider

We all possess a unique ability to do the work we were made for. Concise and easy to read, and including numerous stories of people living on purpose, *The Power of Purpose* is a remarkable tool to help you find your calling, an original guide to discovering the work you love to do.

Hardcover 1997 • ISBN 1-57675-021-3 • Item #50213 $20.00

Paperback 12/04 • ISBN 1-57675-322-0 • Item #53220 $14.95

Second Innocence
Rediscovering Joy and Wonder

John B. Izzo, Ph.D.

Second Innocence describes a unique philosophy for turning life's corners with more enthusiasm, less cynicism, and more faith in each other. The innocence that John Izzo advocates is not the naïve innocence of childhood. This innocence is a chosen one, one that breathes freely despite the scars from life's mistakes and failures, despite the harder truths that become apparent to us as we become adults.

Paperback • ISBN 1-57675-263-1 • Item #52631 $14.95

Berrett-Koehler Publishers
PO Box 565, Williston, VT 05495-9900
Call toll-free! **800-929-2929** 7 am-9 pm EST
Or fax your order to 1-802-864-7626
For fastest service order online: **www.bkconnection.com**

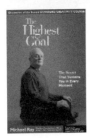

The Highest Goal
The Secret That Sustains You in Every Moment

Michael L. Ray

Throughout the book Ray offers exercises, stories, and reflections that will help you get in touch with your highest goal. He shows us how to open this inner font of creativity, compassion, and courage. Your highest goal is a source of power and wisdom that can vastly improve not only your own life, but the lives of everyone around you.

Hardcover • ISBN 1-57675-286-0 • Item #52860 $24.95

Claiming Your Place at the Fire
Living the Second Half of Your Life on Purpose

Richard Leider and David Shapiro

Bestselling authors Leider and Shapiro present a new paradigm for successful aging for anyone entering into and moving through the second half of their lives, helping them to take their rightful place as "New Elders." This timely book describes how new elders can rekindle the good life, relight the fire within, and share that warmth and light with others.

Paperback • ISBN 1-57675-297-6 • Item #52976 $14.95

Solving Tough Problems
An Open Way of Talking, Listening, and Creating New Realities

Adam Kahane • Foreword by Peter Senge

Kahane worked in the world's hot spots, and came away with a new understanding of how to develop workable solutions even in the most stuck, polarized contexts. In *Solving Tough Problems* Kahane tells his stories and distils from them a "simple but not easy" approach all of us can use to solve our own toughest problems.

Hardcover • ISBN 1-57675-293-3 • Item #52933 $22.95

Berrett-Koehler Publishers
PO Box 565, Williston, VT 05495-9900
Call toll-free! **800-929-2929** 7 am-9 pm EST
Or fax your order to 1-802-864-7626
For fastest service order online: **www.bkconnection.com**

Spread the word!

Berrett-Koehler books are available at quantity discounts for orders of 10 or more copies.

Prisoners of Our Thoughts

Viktor Frankl's Principles at Work

Alex Pattakos

Hardcover
ISBN 1-57675-288-7
Item #52887 $22.95

To find out about discounts for orders of 10 or more copies for individuals, corporations, institutions, and organizations, please call us toll-free at (800) 929-2929.

To find out about our discount programs for resellers, please contact our Special Sales department at (415) 288-0260; Fax: (415) 362-2512. Or email us at bkpub@bkpub.com.

Subscribe to our free e-newsletter!

To find out about what's happening at Berrett-Koehler and to receive announcements of our new books, special offers, free excerpts, and much more, subscribe to our free monthly e-newsletter at www.bkconnection.com.

Berrett-Koehler Publishers
PO Box 565, Williston, VT 05495-9900
Call toll-free! **800-929-2929** 7 am-9 pm EST

Or fax your order to 1-802-864-7626
For fastest service order online: **www.bkconnection.com**